GAGGED

ISBN 978-90-823641-7-0

www.evatasfoundation.com

GAGGED
AMIR VALLE

With an introduction by Ángel Santiesteban Prats

Translated by Jill Powis

CENSORSHIP
IN CUBA

EVATASFOUNDATION

Amsterdam 2016

In Difficult Times

Heberto Padilla,
from *Fuera del Juego* (Sent off the Field) 1968

They asked that man for his time
so they could join it to the time of History.
They asked for his hands,
(...)
They asked for his eyes
(...)
They asked for his lips
(...)
They asked for his legs
(...)
They asked for his chest, his heart, his shoulders.
(...)
Later they explained
that all this giving would be pointless
unless he handed over his tongue,
because in difficult times
there is nothing as useful for stopping hatred and lies.

ETHICS VERSUS REPRESSION AND CENSORSHIP

This is a necessary book because of the unique analysis it provides of the suppression of freedom of expression in Cuba by Fidel Castro's "revolutionary" government. From the triumph of the Cuban Revolution in 1959 to the "Raulist Era" of today, it offers a chilling survey of the most significant cases of cultural repression and censorship perpetrated by the longest Communist dictatorship in the world.

It is also an important book, because it is written by Amir Valle, who has witnessed first hand the oppressive and painful wounds inflicted by censorship and cultural repression. It is therefore not a text written by someone who has coldly studied the issue but rather the honest reflections of a Cuban intellectual, a victim of this censorship and repression – someone who speaks from experience.

Amir Valle was the natural leader of our generation, the group of writers that literary studies call the "Novísimos" [literally, "The Very Latest"]. He was the first of all of us to win national awards and he had the misfortune to suffer censorship before the rest of us, because his work was always critical. He was also the first of us to publicly oppose the regime – most of us were critical in private, but we told him then that he was wrong, that our role was "to write, not to play politics". Although the circumstances were traumatic, he had the good fortune to become, of our generation, the author of the most popular clandestine book in Cuba, 'Habana Babilonia' ('Havana Babylon') about prostitution, and although only around 7 of those 50 writers remain in Cuba, of all of us he was the only one sent into exile in a dirty manoeuvre by the government to remove his bad influence on Cuban intellectuals. He is also one of the exiles most detested by the Castro brothers' dictatorship, because of his ethical stance, his intellectual honesty, his deep knowledge of the reality of political and cultural power in Cuba, and his tireless work as an author and journalist to reveal the sinister truths Castroism wants to conceal from the world.

When colleagues from the Eva Tas Foundation decided to publish this book, Amir wrote to me. "Dear brother, I'm in a dilemma. I have to write a book about the history of cultural censorship. As you know, my case is considered a key example – it should be in that book, but ethically, I can't talk about myself". So we agreed that I would write these words because it is true that any document on the issue in Cuba which excluded the censorship he suffered from his first literary steps until his exile would be incomplete and distorted. I also write these words in gratitude for his generosity. Amir Valle helps any writer who comes to him. Many of the writers of our generation and later generations, well-known today in Cuba and beyond, were his students and a number have even had their books published by international publishing houses as a result of his support. Not only that, when he found out that the Cuban political police had imprisoned me following a show trial to punish me for criticising the dictatorship in my blog 'Los hijos que nadie quiso' ('The children nobody wanted'), Amir, (as well as becoming my unpaid literary agent), joined forces with the Argentinian artist and human rights activist Elisa Tabakman to form a duo to which I owe thanks for raising international awareness of the injustice perpetrated against me and for the vast majority of the expressions of support I have received from cultural and political figures and international institutions.

_ Amir Valle, the trail-blazer...
I met Amir Valle in 1986, at the Alejo Carpentier Centre in Havana, where the Ministry of Culture was holding a National Seminar for Young Writers, which brought together almost all of our generation, the "Novísimos". I was making my first attempts to write when most of those invited had already won awards at the national Literary Workshops. I felt as though I had been plunged into a distant and unknown universe. I had just been released from prison for failing to report my family when they tried to leave the country secretly for the first time. However, what I remember most clearly was my admiration: I regarded them as if they were Nobel Laureates. We had barely introduced ourselves when there was a kind of explosion of affinity, literary interests, emotions. Amir was special: the moment you knew him you liked

him. I was very proud to accept his friendship: at his young age, he was already a legend in the Cuban literary world, someone who made you feel that one day soon he would the great figure of Latin American literature that he is today.

I can safely say, because I witnessed it at first hand, that (with the exception of his first prize and his first book, '*Tiempo en cueros*', ('Time naked'), tales of his childhood in a rural town, published when he was 21) every one of his awards, books and literary and journalistic successes has been a struggle against various forms of censorship, ideological control and cultural repression. In a long interview I had with him in July 2005 when I was still in prison, I forced him to make public many of these struggles against censorship which he had never wanted to talk about. Anyone who reads this interview will reach a clear conclusion: life has rewarded Amir Valle with international prestige, the respect and gratitude of the vast majority of his colleagues, and the fear of his words on the part of the Cuban Revolution's cultural commissars, simply because he has never stopped working, fighting, defending the freedom of his ideas. It has not been easy: in one of our exchanges of messages while I was in prison, he confessed that for every joy during his thirty-year literary career he had received more than a dozen bitter blows. "But I can sleep with a clear conscience, I can look anyone in the eye with my dignity intact and I can say that everything that I have I have won cleanly, far from all those shady secret meetings, literary cliques and ideological and cultural factions that, on all sides of the "Cuban question", live off the suffering of our people," he wrote to me at that time.

I will give this brief summary to give the reader an idea of this difficult intellectual journey:

In 1983, aged 16, he joined the Literary Workshops Movement in Santiago de Cuba, which at that time were very important. By 1984 his problems were already beginning. He conceived and founded, with other young writers, a literary group, "Seis del Ochenta" ("Six of the Eighty"), which immediately received threats from the censors, as in their manifesto they announced that they intended to write about "taboo and problematic subjects relating to Cuban reality". All its members were "warned" by the political police that their ideas could be exploited by the enemies of the revolution, and counterintelligence officials planted a spy in their ranks (another young writer). Due to the critical nature of their stories, it was José Mariano Torralbas and Amir who suffered the severest censorship. They were put on a blacklist that would force Torralbas to emigrate when all doors were closed to him in Cuba; it was a blacklist that Amir would never be taken off.

In 1987, there was another daring act: he submitted 'Cambiar' ('Change'), a short story, for the national award of 'Muchacha', one of Cuba's most important magazines. Thanks to a courageous jury, he won the competition and after a hard fight against the censors, writer Waldo González López, the organiser of the award, managed to get the story published. It tackled a highly sensitive issue: the double standards and ideological manipulation of young Cubans through the Communist Youth League (UJC), an appendage the Communist Party. That put him back in the crosshairs of those who already considered him an "ideological deviant". I witnessed how officers from State Security (political police) interrupted the class at the Faculty of Journalism and took him out of the classroom for questioning, asking him to account for comments he had made at cultural venues or in private, which made us realise that he was being kept under constant surveillance.

Thus would begin a shameful succession of acts of censorship of his work. In Cuba, these processes are usually secret and authors almost never manage to prove that they have been censored, but the affection and respect that Amir had gained allowed many of us to find out about the ploys being used to silence his criticism: in most cases, the censors themselves (writers or state officials) leaked us the information, admitting that they were forced to censor him.

A few examples:
- 'Yo soy el malo' ('I am the villain'), the book with which Amir won second place in 1986 in the important David Prize, awarded by the National Union of Writers and Artists of Cuba (UNEAC). It would be published three years later, after a long battle with the censors;

- Due to his public condemnation of the censorship of 'Yo soy el malo', there were threats that 'En el nombre de Dios' ('In the name of God') would be stripped of the award that he had won for the book in 1988, UNEAC's Testimonial Narratives Prize, the most important of its kind in the country. This was prevented by the strong opposition of a member of UNEAC's board, the writer Vasco Justo, supported by other writers. The book was published in 1990, two years later;
- his book 'Manuscritos del muerto' ('Manuscripts of the dead'), a novella about the censorship of a journalist in a country dominated by a dictator (one of five finalists for the Casa de las Américas Award in 1994), would see the light of day in 2000, totally butchered, after the political police sent the writer Eduardo Heras León (our teacher and mentor, almost a father to us) to convince him of the "need" to remove the critical parts of the book. Amir accepted the butchery of his work out of respect for the teacher;
- his short story 'Mambrú no fue a la guerra' ('Mambrú did not go to war'), a uncompromising account of the true story of a Cuban soldier maimed in Cuba's internationalist wars in Africa. There were moves to exclude it from 'Aire de Luz' ('Air of Light'), an anthology of the best Cuban stories of the twentieth century, selected by the writer Alberto Garrandés. Luckily, the anthologist refused, warned other selected writers and we all made it known to the censors that we would not allow our short stories to be published if Amir was excluded.
- from 1990 to 1999, no Cuban publishing house would accept his books, despite his being recognised by literary critics as one of the country's most distinguished writers.

from 2000 to 2005, except for the erotic fantasy novels 'Muchacha azul bajo la lluvia' ('Blue girl in the rain'), 'Los desnudos de Dios' ('The naked of God') and the noir novel 'Si Cristo te desnuda' ('If Christ undressed you') (which had to be published because they won national awards, and the prize was publication), Cuban publishers censored 'Las puertas de la noche' ('The portals of night'), 'Entre el miedo y las sombras' ('Between fear and shadows'), and 'Santuario de sombras' ('Sanctuary of shadows'), all of them dealing with Cuban lives on the margins of society. It was precisely with these novels that Amir Valle achieved international recognition, when they were published in several languages by major European publishing companies.

These acts of censorship dragged down Amir's hopes; something changed radically in him. It was a cruel farewell to the naivety that many of us still retained and, with the precocity that he always had, he decided to distance himself from official spaces. I confess that I was one of those did not understand it then; mistakenly, I thought that it was enough to be producing critical, social and anti-government literature. That was what we were taught by our teachers who had allowed their generation to be crushed by fear, a fear that they then tried to transmit to us so that we would not suffer the repression they experienced in the !960s and 1970s. I remember that when Amir clearly told me about his opposition to the totalitarian regime, his severe criticisms of the dictatorship and the human rights violations in Cuba, due to my political immaturity and the manipulation I had not yet escaped, I told him that "as an artist you shouldn't get confused about our weapon – it's literature. Our role is to write, not to play politics".

_ Havana Babylon, Cuban censorship's biggest blunder
Amir Valle is the author of what is believed to be the biggest underground bestseller in the history of Cuban literature: 'Havana Babylon', an in-depth investigation which ranges from the first historical evidence of prostitution on the island to its re-emergence with Cuba's economic crisis following the fall of Communism in Russia and Europe. After graduating in journalism from the University of Havana in 1989, he spent several years inside the world of prostitution and poverty to write this book. Years later, following its publication by Editorial Planeta in 2006, it won the prestigious international Rodolfo Walsh Prize, awarded each year to the best non-fiction book published in the Spanish language. It is regarded by critics as a classic of the genre in Latin America and there are dozens of doctorates and theses on this work.

However, in Cuba it had to be distributed clandestinely in the years before it was finally published (no Cuban publishing house has as yet done so). In 1999, after five years of work, Amir decided to submit it for the Casa de las Américas Prize, in the Testimonial Narratives category. Around that time, writers of our generation were attending a workshop in Havana and witnessed something that made us proud – two of our own, Alberto Garrido and Amir Valle, won the prize in the short story and testimonial narrative categories, respectively. Years later we would learn something that Amir would not tell us at that time, out of concern for those who gave him the evidence: there was manipulation of the jury against his work. One of the jurors (who vetoed it saying the book was not appropriate given the problems facing the country) reported it to the political police and, even though Amir was informed unofficially that he had won, the prize was not awarded to him. I witnessed the news spreading throughout Havana that Amir had been stripped of the prize. At the awards ceremony, when the chair of the jury read out the results and declared the prize void, we booed in protest, which caught the attention of the audience and the foreign press. The next day, the foreign media wrote, "A Cuban is stripped of Casa de las Américas Prize for political reasons".

How did that unpublished book become an underground bestseller? In 2004, after a lot of research, Amir's German literary agent, Ray Güde Mertin, found out that someone had photocopied one of the copies sent for the prize, turned it into a Word document and put it on a CD which was circulated round the island in 2000 along with other banned works, including 'Before Night Falls' by Reinaldo Arenas, some books by Mario Vargas Llosa and 'Castro's Final Hour' by Andrés Oppenheimer. It was also around that time that the email system controlled through the "intranet" began (a type of internet just for Cuba, without access to the real open internet), which meant that circulation of the text went viral.

The attempt to censor the book by withdrawing the prize became its biggest promoter: during that first stage, it reached thousands of Cuban readers. The cultural and political authorities began a silent campaign against it in workplaces all over in the country. "A counter-revolutionary document is being circulated" was the slogan of that campaign which would attract even more readers. Unfortunately, it also caused sackings and other "acts of repudiation" of workers who had been discovered printing or copying a text deemed "an enemy of the Revolution". Finally, after the book was published in 2006, with Amir now living in exile in Germany, Fidel Castro himself attacked the work in response to the international publicity it was gaining, branding a Cuban journalist emigre who interviewed Amir and, days later, the author himself as "*jineterólogos*" ("hooker experts"). This was the boost needed for Cubans to embark en masse on a hunt for the book that, to this day, is still an underground bestseller desperately sought after by new generations of Cubans.

_ The Cuban Culture Collection: another blow from censorship
The cultural authorities and the political police monitoring culture would be attacked by a fresh wave of anger when, in 2002, Amir Valle decided to take over responsibility for the single most important opposition event at Cuba's International Book Fair to this day: presentations of the Cuban Culture Collection of *Plaza Mayor*, the Puerto Rican publishing house.

The official cultural policy faced two challenges: first, the Collection would publish (and would present both within Cuba and outside Cuba) authors from both sides, trying to break down the wall with which the Revolution divided Cuban writers on the island and in exile; and second, the project was managed by Patricia Gutiérrez-Menoyo, daughter of one of the legendary guerrilla rebels, former comrades-in-arms of Fidel Castro: Eloy Gutiérrez Menoyo, who was one of the first leaders to actively oppose the Communist direction the Revolution had taken.

These were years when Cuban cultural policy strategists had convinced Fidel Castro of the need to present an image of openness to the world. Thus began a strategy to regain the international support of left-wing intellectuals who had distanced themselves from the Revolution for two decades because of the undeniable cultural repression on the island since the so-called

"Padilla Affair" in 1971. The publication of books by less critical foreign writers began to be permitted, national publishing houses began publishing exiled Cuban writers (if they did not have a very critical stance against the Revolution), the work of some Cuban writers who had died in exile was published, and Cuban magazines could include references to the work of authors, artists, musicians and intellectuals which had been totally banned for decades. It was through that strategy that there was approval for the presence at the International Book Fair of Patricia, the publisher, in 2000 and, from 2002, official presentations of the titles that she would begin to publish.

It was in 2002 that Amir Valle became Plaza Mayor's Coordinator in Cuba, which intensified attacks by the censors, who tried and failed to get it to comply with its demands: to moderate language critical of the government's segregationist cultural policy in its promotional material and to not publish counter-revolutionary authors. As it was a means of being published outside Cuba (an opportunity the government only granted to a few authors in exchange for their services as mouthpieces for the Revolution), most Cuban writers gravitated towards Amir and the work he was doing for Plaza Mayor from his home in central Havana; work in many fields which resulted in the publication of 30 titles (24 of them personally managed by Amir) and in two prizes for novels which could be awarded to authors on the island and in exile.

In May 2002, Abel Prieto, the Minister of Culture, launched a campaign at a national meeting of the ministry to discredit the project and its Coordinator, in view of Amir's refusal to apply the censorship to the Cuban Culture Collection demanded by the cultural authorities. In a subsequent meeting, the Minister would issue the order that Amir should not be employed in any cultural institution, should not be given any promotional opportunities, nor should his books be published or his works included in anthologies or national magazines. Despite this, that same year, Cuba was Guest of Honour at the Guadalajara International Book Fair and, after much negotiation, in an attempt to project an image of tolerance, the Cuban delegation agreed to include the Collection and several of its authors, both resident on the island and in exile.

This stifling atmosphere, which converted Amir into a social outcast, someone whom nobody should approach to "avoid being contaminated", became even more suffocating when in 2003, the commander Eloy Gutiérrez Menoyo, who had been living in Miami since 1986, exercised his rights as a Spanish citizen who was a naturalised Cuban, and decided to return to Cuba to demand legal status for his political group, *Cambio Cubano* (Cuban Change). He made daily visits to Amir's home; the political police declared Amir a "collaborator with the enemy" and, to closely monitor their movements, they used writer Raúl Antonio Capote (agent "Daniel") as a spy, taking advantage of the friendship and close personal relationship the two authors had shared from very young.

By 2004 the regime had decided to stop such a corrupting project because, despite all the attacks and all the propaganda deployed against it, the Cuban Culture Collection continued to gain admirers and support among Cuban intellectuals, both on the island and in exile. The 2004 Havana International Book Fair would eventually provide the pretext: during the presentation of the latest titles, with the room full of people, Patricia Gutiérrez Menoyo launched into a speech that was too critical and provocative for the censors' taste. In that speech, the publisher condemned the countless obstacles faced by the project: changes of site and programme without notice, disinformation to confuse readers, delays in customs procedures to prevent the books reaching the fair, threats to Cuba-based authors and the ban on the exiled writer, Luis Manuel García, from travelling to Cuba to present his book of short stories 'El *éxito del tigre*' ('Success of the Tiger'). Patricia said that such a ban was due to the fact that this writer, who lives in Spain, was also editor of the magazine 'Encuentro *de la Cultura Cubana*' ('Encounter with Cuban Culture', banned in Cuba). She read to those present a message of condemnation sent by Luis Manuel from Madrid and another letter from Sweden, sent by the Cuban novelist Antonio Álvarez Gil, who clearly stated that he was refusing to come to Cuba to show solidarity with his colleague Luis Manuel and the 75 journalists imprisoned during the "Black Spring" of 2003 for the sole "crime" of informing the world of truths that the dictatorship tried to conceal.

Repressive measures were not long in coming: they needed to completely silence Amir Valle, as doing so would sever the influence of Patricia Gutiérrez Menoyo's publishing project on Cuban intellectuals. On 3 February 2005, days before the start of a new season of the Fair, to which the Collection had not been invited, the Cubarte network (a server that provides email services to Cuban artists and writers) informed Amir, "We've been checking on the misuse of email to disseminate information which is not in line with the interests of the Cubarte network and therefore we have decided to suspend you from this service". The "misuse" to which they referred was the magazine 'Letras en Cuba' ('Literature in Cuba'), an independent publication that Amir drafted, designed and sent to thousands of readers outside the island via email, because he was never granted direct access to the internet. In the end, there were 30 editions of 'Letras en Cuba' and it was published at a time when there was no other Cuban literary magazine on the internet. After weeks of legal wrangling, he was once again connected to the email service, but only on condition that it would be used for personal matters and never to issue unauthorised publications. Amir then created a system of "information capsules" (small news items on important cultural developments not covered by the official press), calling them 'A título personal' ('In a personal capacity'). He only managed to send out three capsules before the Ministry of Culture ordered that he should be totally denied access to email. As a result, until his departure from Cuba, he was forced to rent pirate accounts on the island's internet black market.

_ Removing the rotten apple from the barrel
However, as I said at the beginning, Amir's constant work helping young writers, giving workshops in various parts of the city and in his own home, the years when he was on the fiction panel of many of the most important events throughout the island, the three years (1995-1998) when he worked in the Literature Department of the Cuban Book Institute dealing with writers from all over the country, the two national courses that he taught

as a professor of narrative technique at the Onelio Jorge Cardoso National Literary Training Centre, his work as General Coordinator of Plaza Mayor's Cuban Culture Collection, the silent admiration that most of his colleagues from several generations felt for his ethical stance towards the government (saying what many of us wanted but did not dare to say about the situation in the country), and the bans on his work that only increased Cuban readers' desire to know his books, his writings, his views, made him one of the most influential Cuban writers within the Cuban intelligentsia in those years. Furthermore, since the publication in 2001 in Spain of his novel 'The portals of night', on a real case of child prostitution in Cuba, the international press often interviewed him, his books began to win the most prestigious European critics' and readers' awards, and that gave his criticism of the government even more impact.

Arresting him, as they had done with other journalists and writers with a lower or non-existent international profile, would have been too damaging to the image of "tolerance" that the Revolution was trying to project. It was therefore decided to sever his influence over the Cuban intellectual and cultural world, especially on the younger generations of writers. As we later learned, at that time Abel Prieto, the Minister of Culture, commented to a colleague on the dirty trick he had devised, "Amir is a rotten apple and rotten apples are thrown out of the barrel so that they don't rot the others".

In October 2005, Amir went to Spain on a book tour to publicise his novel 'Sanctuary of shadows' on another taboo subject at that time in Cuba – human trafficking by sea to the United States with the collusion of members of the Cuban military. When he finished the tour, the authorities prevented him from re-entering the island. After staying illegally in Spain for several months, his German publisher got him a scholarship at the Heinrich Böll Foundation for six months. After that, when it was obvious that the Cuban government had not responded to the international campaign demanding the return of Amir to the island, the PEN Club of Germany awarded him a grant under the Writers in Exile international programme for three years. In 2009, as he was unable to return to Cuba, the German authorities granted him political asylum. Even today his name is on a blacklist of Cubans who, according to the dictatorship, have lost the right to return to Cuba. As if it were not enough to exile him for 10 years from his homeland and from the cultural scene where, fortunately, he is still admired and respected, in early 2015, the regime sent a cultural commissar (an old friend from his youth, whom Amir agreed to meet through pure nostalgia for the good times) to tell him that if he wanted to visit or return to the island, it would be advisable, at the very least, to tone down his criticism. "If you kept quiet for a while, they'd examine the possibility of letting you in at some point. It'd be wise for you to adapt to the new era brought in by the talks between Obama and Raúl," said the commissar. Amir's response has been clear: 2015 was the year when, through his work as a journalist for major German, Spanish and Latin American media outlets, he even more actively denounced the farce of "change" and dialogue with the enemy through which the Castroists are seeking to transfer all their power to their heirs, the Neo-Castroists.

This is the writer and journalist whose vision of censorship in Cuba you will read in this book. In both fields, literature and journalism, he has had many bitter experiences, confronting censors and repressors, and therefore his voice is important and his experience necessary to build that future free Cuba to which we all aspire. A Cuba where Culture will have to rebuild its historic, true pillars – ethical, libertarian and inclusive – destroyed by the ideology-driven cultural policy of this monster called the "Cuban Revolution".

Ángel Santiesteban Prats

CHAPTER I
THE BEAST AWAKES

"None of us who fought alongside Fidel had enough vision to escape his personality, although many had already seen signs that a future government led by him would be anything but democratic. However, in those early years, still very close in time to the amazing popular euphoria of the 1959 victory, the beast of authoritarianism was still drowsy after swallowing up the past we had fought against," said writer and journalist Carlos Franqui (Cuba, 1921 – Puerto Rico, 2010) in a 2007 interview. From the time of Sierra Maestra until shortly after the triumph of the Cuban Revolution in 1959, he had been drafted in by Fidel Castro to head up the '*Revolución*' ('Revolution') newspaper and *Radio Rebelde* (Rebel Radio), official media outlets of the 26th of July Movement that defeated the dictator Fulgencio Batista.

This seems to be an eternal truth: all revolutions blind their children with the euphoria of victory – or at least, at the beginning of that victory. Cuba, before 1959, was not the total chaos that the official version of history would later depict; a false and manipulative account of reality which many still believe. It is sufficient to read Fidel Castro's own assessment of the economic, political and social situation in Cuba in his defence speech at his trial in 1953, known as 'History Will Absolve Me', officially considered the Economic and Social Programme of the Revolution, to see that the Cuba of today, after 57 years, is more unequal and more economically, financially and socially impoverished than the Cuba that he began to govern on 1 January 1959. Cuba, in 1958, was a nation in full economic development. Its financial system was among the strongest in Latin America (just one example – the Cuban peso had the same value as the dollar) and, besides being one of the most advanced nations in the world in terms of telephony, communications and transport, the island was considered by every international organisation as a model of development, including in terms of education and public health (the two "legendary successes" of revolutionary propaganda). The only real difference between the Cuba of 1958 and 2015 "in favour" of the Revolution lies in the unfulfilled promises of revolutionary rhetoric: that more prosperous country, that nation of greater dignity, that real equality among all Cubans, that absolute independence in all areas of life that Cubans still seek but do not find.

However, it was undeniable that profound changes were needed in Cuba. There were major social problems to resolve; there was political corruption, the scale of which hardly varied from government to government; there was a servile relationship with US administrations (which, although in some periods had been a shameful dependency, this had been diminishing as the nation gradually gained economic and financial independence); Batista's coup in 1952 had attacked the pillars of state which Cubans were proud of (democracy, the separation of powers and a constitution which, at that time, was considered one of the most progressive in the world) and finally, the dictator Batista's decision to give free rein to his repressive forces to try and curb growing social discontent, permitting the physical extermination of opposition groups, mostly composed of young people who started to be tortured and killed in many cities, all led to a rose-tinted view of "Dr. Castro and his bearded men". Fidel saw himself as a Messiah who would save the Cuban people. Against this background, the Cuban people's euphoric – and in many senses blind and deaf – support for the triumphant Revolution was natural in those early days.

Note that I say "blind and deaf support" because, when I mentioned Franqui's words to another of those legendary bearded men, Commander Huber Matos (Cuba, 1918 – Miami, 2014), he would tell me in an interview in 2009, "You can't say that nobody had the vision to foresee totalitarianism. There were many who, even before victory, dared to warn about the dangers looming ahead, not only from the Communists' manoeuvres, but also the potentially serious problems for democracy and freedom presented by the combination of Communist influence and Fidel's authoritarian and egotistical personality within the same arena of power. It wasn't that we didn't have vision; it was rather that we didn't *want* to see or hear. As I've said many times, even though I was one of the first to be punished for opposing the change of course, before I hadn't paid much attention to compatriots and friends who had commented on it to me".

In Berlin, in a conversation in 2011 with the best-known Cuban journalist, Carlos Alberto Montaner, also an author, we exchanged views on the opposition's mobilisation on the island. I noticed that we both referred to the same issue, vital for the development of a society – free access to information. We agreed that, when he discovered that he had failed in his strategy of exerting control over the Cuban political scene by associating himself with gangster organisations, behaving in an openly Mafia-like way, Fidel Castro instead advocated proselytism which, exploiting his rhetorical skills and his wide reading, acquired a strongly intellectual flavour. It was precisely this knowledge of the power of words to raise consciousness and the experience of all the damage the free press had inflicted on Batista (Fidel himself wrote opposing the dictatorship using newspapers of the time), coupled with his innate incapacity for dialogue which made him want to be the sole authority on any matter, which enabled him to understand that he could not monopolise power if he allowed freedom of the press. Journalism was of no use to Fidel Castro; he knew perfectly well that when the media is in the hands of a single power, journalism ends and propaganda begins: and that was just what he needed.

> "First the Revolution and then the newspaper. The interests of the newspaper must be subordinated to the interests of the Revolution."
> (Fidel Castro, Revolución, 27 March 1961, p. 5)

To understand the radical nature of censorship in Cuba, one has to examine the level of development of journalism and freedom of information that Fidel Castro found there when he assumed power in 1959. According to reports by international organisations and experts, in Latin America the island was second only to the United States and was one of the most developed countries in the world in this field. With a population of little over 6 million,

Cuba had 58 newspapers (now there are barely 20 for 11 million Cubans), 126 magazines (today, only about 30), 160 radio stations (now there are only around 20 in operation) and 600 cinemas (only Havana had more cinemas than New York, but according to recent statistics barely 36 survive throughout the island, in poor condition). We also had the most modern television in the Latin America after the United States and, most importantly, all political tendencies and religious and spiritual beliefs had their own press media.

However now, according to a 2014 report by the International Federation of Journalists, Cuba is the most backward country in the region in terms of the technological development of the media and on-line information, and all the reports by Reporters Without Borders and the Inter-American Press Association over the past five years name Cuba as one of the countries with most restrictions and violations of press freedom in the world.

It is not, therefore, solely a question of control of the media. It is the monopolisation of discourse by one voice, eliminating journalism and establishing propaganda as the only means of communication and source of information for the people. It is the concentration of publishing houses in the hands of the revolutionary government (there are no independent publishers outside state control). It is the nationalisation of all radio and TV stations, as well as all telephone networks. It is the rewriting the nation's history to favour the "revolutionary present", presenting a bleak vision of Cuba that only the revolution's social project could change. This process began just a few months after victory, when the media got back to normal after the collective national euphoria that converted all newspapers, radio and television stations into a chorus applauding the arrival of a new era for the Cuban people. It had just started to very mildly criticise the revolutionary government, when Fidel Castro exploded in anger and began to restrict journalists' freedoms, taking over newspapers, harshly attacking the most important political commentators opposing him, launching smear campaigns to deceive the people about the integrity of journalists and media outlets which had a lot of popular support (basically accusing them of defending the hated Batista era). In 1965 he dealt the death blow to freedom of the press and journalism by creating two important icons of official propaganda: the newspapers 'Granma' (official mouthpiece of the Communist Party of Cuba) and 'Juventud Rebelde' (the official newspaper of the UJC).

From that time onwards, no news has been published in Cuba without the prior approval of a control structure known as the Department of Revolutionary Orientation (DOR), an agency of the Central Committee of the Communist Party. It is responsible for centralising and monitoring all information circulating on the island; no melody that has been banned by these censors can be broadcast; no literary, historical, scientific or other book can be published unless it has the vote of the various inspection departments embedded in the country's ministries; no documentary or film can be screened unless it meets the rigid requirements of the so-called "Cultural Policy of the Revolution". Furthermore, as is well known, the fact that one company has the monopoly on telecommunications (ETECSA, which has a Department of Cybernetic Espionage which reports to the Ministry of the Interior), means that even private telephone and email messages can be monitored.

Information, in essence, is one of the powers most energetically defended by the dictatorship, although there have been some very interesting strategic changes since Raúl Castro assumed power in 2006, which aim to present to the world an image of openness and respect for freedom of information and opinion. In simple terms, it is yet one more among the many times that, to continue Carlos Franqui's analogy at the beginning of this chapter, the beast of Castro's censorship has had to shed its skin since waking from its slumber – changes of skin which are nothing more than changes in strategy to adapt to the new global context, the swampy ideological times and the fresh international challenges facing the "Revolution, beacon of light to the poor of the world", so that nobody will discover the truth behind that mask.

_ 1959-1971 – The remnants of capitalism

As early as 1959, in an attempt to control, from within the press itself, any news critical of the government, "Press Freedom Committees" were set up, responsible for demonstrating to the people that "the workers, the poor people, that is, revolutionary journalists" disagreed with the editorial policies of the "capitalist" newspaper owners, using the method known as "coletillas" (tags), short texts that were printed, against the editors' will, next to any news criticising the Revolution.

Not one newspaper escaped these coletillas. In his book La imposición del silencio: Cómo se clausuró la libertad de prensa en Cuba ('The imposition of silence: How press freedom was shut down in Cuba'), the journalist Waldo Fernández Cuenca quotes one of the most representative:

"This section is published freely by this newspaper company exercising the freedom of the press which exists in Cuba, but the Local Press Freedom Committee of Journalists and Photographers of this workplace states, also in the legitimate exercise of that right, that they do not share the views expressed by the author and published in this section. The sole fact of preferring to read texts which praise Díaz Lanz, Pedraza, Ventura and other murderers and traitors to the homeland, in which the current regime in Cuba is put in the same category as the brutal regimes of Santo Domingo, Nicaragua and Paraguay, is clearly saying that the author would happily join that vile chorus of loud-mouths screaming, "Long live chains!" ('Una carta con sobre' ('A letter with an envelope') in Diario de la Marina, 22 March 1960, p. 4).

Although the coletillas were short-lived, because they usually ended when the newspaper or magazine was taken over by the revolutionary regime, the practice was transferred to publishing and there were many books published with a loose sheet, in the style of erratas, which provided "revolutionary clarifications". The most notorious example was the book at the heart of the explosive Padilla Affair, discussed in the next chapter. Padilla's poetry collection 'Fuera del juego' ('Sent off the field'), which won the 1968 Julián del Casal Prize awarded by UNEAC, was published with a note which expressed disagreement with the prize and with the work itself, as it was considered ideologically opposed to the Revolution. The note included the claim that Padilla:

> "maintains two basic attitudes: one critical and the other antihistorical. His criticism is exercised from a distance that is not the active engagement that characterises revolutionaries. (...) His antihistoricism is expressed through the exaltation of individualism in the face of the collective demands of the people (...). Both attitudes have always been typical of the thinking of the right, and have traditionally served as an instrument of the counter-revolution".

Although there were other variants of "revolutionary" censorship, note that both the coletillas and these sheets accompanying books, as well as the attacks that Fidel Castro and the intellectuals in his service launched against renowned journalists, writers and broadcasters in those years, all formed part of a clear censorship strategy with propagandist overtones: accuse anyone who makes any kind of criticism of supporting the defeated enemy, that is, the dictator Fulgencio Batista and any of the "capitalist remnants" that he and his defeated government represented for the collective memory of the Cuban people.

These so-called "remnants of capitalism" that, according to the poisonous logic of the "revolutionary" censors and repressors, shackled many Cubans to the Batista past, served as the pretext for taking over the country's media outlets; for censoring films (the best known case being 'PM', by Sabá Cabrera Infante and Orlando Jiménez Leal, a portrait of Havana at night, in which parties and liquor, according to the censors, depicted a Cuba that had been left behind); for closing the cultural supplement 'Lunes de Revolución'; for marginalising José Lezama Lima, Virgilio Piñera and other significant intellectual figures who, according to Mirtha Aguirre, a Communist cultural commissar, "were still shut away in their ivory towers, far from the heroic everyday life of the people"; for persecuting thousands of artists and intellectuals because of their "improper" or "indecent" or "unnatural" sexual inclinations and locking up hundreds of them in concentration camps called UMAP (Military Units to Aid Production); for censoring writers and literary groups (the best known example being El Puente group) for failing to produce literature, "in line with the new times and the new men we want to build" (as the censor Luis Pavón Tamayo liked to repeat in his articles published under a pseudonym in the Revolutionary Armed Forces' magazine 'Verde Olivo' ('Olive Green')), even for imprisoning over a dozen young writers, and finally, although with indications of a change in this strategy of censorship and repression, for convicting the poet Heberto Padilla and forcing him into exile.

It was enough for Fidel Castro to insinuate that any critics were Batista collaborators for the population to want to take the law into their own hands. Then, assuming the role of vigilantes responding "to the genuine outrage of our revolutionary people", the government could carry out censorship, repression, nationalisation, exile and even executions, with the blessing of the masses. This propaganda had a single purpose: to get the people to shout, as so many did in those years, "Against the wall! Against the wall! Against the wall!" unknowingly legitimising with their cries the future death of their own individual liberties.

_ 1971-1989 The betrayal of the people of the Revolution
In this period, Fidel Castro suffered two major setbacks which in many ways can be regarded as responsible for the change in the government strategy of censorship and repression. It was the end of a decade in which the world's eyes were on Cuba: the process led by Fidel was a beacon of light, seemingly a more national, more indigenous, purer socialism than Russia had imposed on the countries of Eastern Europe after the defeat of Hitler. This revival of revolutionary purity that many saw in the Cuban Revolution was happening at a time when the militaristic polarisation of the conflict between US imperialism and Soviet imperialism was dissolving, for well-known reasons, including the obvious errors of socialism à la Soviet and the notorious failure of the international socialist economy.

The first setback, according to the protagonists themselves, comrades-in-arms of Fidel Castro, deepened the radicalism and blind obstinacy of the already-dubbed "Supreme Leader". He got it into his head that the domestic sugar industry could produce 10 million tonnes of sugar, spurred by the commitment by the Soviet president, Nikita Khrushchev, to buy up to five million tonnes of sugar from Cuba at preferential prices. A range of experts warned him that all the sugar mills in the country combined were only technically capable of producing 7 and a half million tonnes. Castro's response was the same as always: he sacked those officials "who had no faith in the power of the Revolution" and he ordered all the country's resources to be devoted to the task. As the sacked experts predicted, barely 8 million tonnes was reached, at an absurd economic cost.

The second setback, according to Chilean writer and journalist Jorge Edwards, when I interviewed him in Berlin in 2015, "was a harder blow. Fidel was very confident that he had a lot of arguments to justify the defeats he was suffering during those years on the economic front, but he wasn't willing to lose ground on the ideological front, and the Padilla Affair is, without question, the most serious ideological wound received by the Revolution in its entire existence, because it took away one of its most effective propaganda weapons: the monopoly it had once had over the international intelligentsia".

As will be explained later, following the repression against Heberto Padilla (extended to other writers after the Stalinist purge-style speech of self-incrimination that he was forced to make, accusing colleagues of being too weak in the face of "the great epic of the Revolution"), most international left-wing intellectuals, especially in Latin America, had their eyes opened to the signs of totalitarianism in the revolutionary government and they publicly broke off relations with Havana.

One important detail can not be overlooked: from 1970, it became increasingly clear that Fidel Castro wished to become "the world leader of the exploited", using his status as the leader of "the first victory of the peoples of America against world imperialism" and of the "first major defeat in Latin America" for the United States, during the Bay of Pigs invasion in

1961. At the same time, the Soviet empire was beginning to take a direct interest in the guerrilla movements in Central and South America and needed a pawn. As a result, according to experts on Soviet expansionism, Moscow decided to help secure a leadership role for Fidel Castro on the world stage, putting aside the differences which had arisen between the two governments through the Soviet decision to sit down and negotiate with the United States, behind Fidel's back, about the presence of Russian nuclear weapons on Cuban soil during the Missile Crisis in October 1962.

All international socialist propaganda therefore became focused on promoting the Non-Aligned Movement (NAM), because although it was politically independent on paper, in practice it was Moscow's most viable diplomatic option for confronting "world imperialism". It is highly significant that it carried out relentless lobbying, directly or through its satellites within the Movement, to secure a leadership role for Fidel Castro. It began with NAM's Sixth Summit, which was held in Havana, and was consolidated between 1980 and 1985 with the international importance the whole socialist bloc accorded to one of Fidel's most "anti-capitalist" ideas: his declarations that neither the foreign debt of Latin America, nor of other poor countries, should be paid, because it was the creditor nations who were responsible for the poverty and plunder of the Third World.

Within this new context, in the face of these new challenges for the international left and the Revolution, censorship and repression of ideas could no longer be justified with the old labels of "remnants of capitalism" or "defenders of the Batista past". Both in Fidel's declarations in response to the intellectuals who demonstrated against the repression of Heberto Padilla, and in open letters by Cuban intellectuals that the revolutionary government used to respond to what it considered a stab in the back, the idea of betrayal began to come to the fore, with propaganda focused on labelling foreign critics as "traitors to the ideals of the International Revolution of the dispossessed", and branding Cuban critics as "traitors to the revolutionary people", using labels (although they were used before in some cases) such as "rats", "unpatriotic", "hostile to the Revolution", "ideological deviants" and "gusanos" ("worms") or "escorias" ("scum"). These latter names were used with a lot more force following the mass exodus of 1980, when over 125,000 Cubans decided to leave the island through Mariel port and the government ordered the so-called "acts of repudiation" (still in existence to this day) whereby massed demonstrators, among many other insults, shouted at those who asked leave the country a sadly well-known chorus: *Pin Pon Fuera, Abajo la Gusanera!* (Pin Pon Out, Down with the Maggots' Nest!).

To impose his leadership, Fidel Castro could not afford scandals such as the Padilla Affair, or complaints about methods of repression such as the "UMAP Concentration Camps". He therefore ordered the control mechanisms to be adjusted through the extensive network of State Security informants and the presence of the political police in all work and social spaces on the island, while commanding his intellectual commissars to implement a cultural strategy that would simultaneously promote and develop culture, bringing it to the masses, while maintaining it under the strict control of government bodies.

Although some cases of censorship and repression managed to escape the siege of international silence imposed by the Cuban government, censorship and repression became subtler. It became specialised, it concentrated on projecting the image of an island where the people enjoyed a wide range of opportunities for cultural development. Therefore, even though it is possible to speak of other Padilla Affairs in this period, with the exception of the international publicity gained by the treatment of the writer Reinaldo Arenas (Holguín, Cuba, 1943 – New York, 1990), the terrible situation for the rest of the repressed writers is little known, even when that repression was much worse than that perpetrated against Heberto Padilla.

_ 1990-2003 – The mercenaries of the Empire
The fall of the Berlin Wall in November 1989 and the break-up of the Soviet empire in Russia and other Eastern European countries soon after forced the government to adopt new strategies in all areas of its administration. The abrupt halt to the generous Soviet subsidies to a Cuban economy which depended for even the most basic supplies on Moscow's "solidarity", meant

that the country was facing a total crisis that Fidel Castro, deploying one of his usual euphemisms, called a "Special Period in Time of Peace", marking the beginning of one of the darkest phases of the revolutionary period: severe shortages of food (not even the distribution of rations was assured, through "supply books" which should have provided every Cuban family with a basic diet at state-subsidised prices), medicines and hospital supplies and equipment (starting the total decline in what had been achieved in public health in previous years), oil (the people called that period "el gran alumbrón" ("the great illumination") because rare was the day when there were no power cuts) and the shortage or absence of all kinds of resources for domestic industry, including tourism.

In parallel, the United States stepped up its attacks on the Cuban government, almost convinced that Fidel Castro would not survive much longer. It intensified espionage against the island, conducted military exercises, rehearsed airstrikes and tried to get the Cuban regime condemned at the UN Human Rights Commission. This new escalation was interpreted by Cuba as the prelude to a potential direct attack, and it responded by fortifying its defence system with the concept of the "War of All the People" (every Cuban, according to this concept, should have a place, a method and the means of countering this imperialist attack).

As well as all the international pressure on Cuba, condemned as the last country to cling to a system evidently in its death throes, in 1990 former President George Bush (senior) added the broadcasts of Television Martí to those of Radio Martí, set up in 1983 by Ronald Reagan to bombard the island with programmes to open Cubans' eyes to the truths that the regime concealed from them, protected by its media monopoly. As if this act of "aggression" were not enough, although TV Martí can now be watched on the island thanks to the Hispasat satellite, initially it broadcast from an aerostat balloon 3,000 metres above the Florida Keys. However, when it failed to achieve the expected range, an airborne transmitter was used. In 2004 and 2005, this was a C-130 Hercules military plane which flew along the Florida Straits and belonged to one of the Pentagon's psychological warfare units (which Fidel Castro pointed to as another sign of an impending attack).

32

It was precisely in this period, seeking the information that the official media failed to supply, that Cubans began using a vast network of homebuilt satellite dishes and secret cables which "stole" the television signals of hotels and tourist and government facilities (forbidden to Cubans). Also in those years, specifically from 1985, a lot of literature circulated in Cuba, via underground routes, which examined how, beginning with *perestroika* (restructuring) and later through *glasnost* (openness), Eastern Europe's socialist system was collapsing from within.

The first sign that Fidel Castro would never allow either *perestroika* or *glasnost* was when, as journalism students at Havana University, we requested a meeting with him in October 1987. For the first time, he was asked very uncomfortable questions about, for example, press freedom, the monopoly on information, authoritarianism within the revolutionary elite, and the gross exaggeration of revolutionary targets. One of Fidel's essential clarifications at that meeting was to stress (three years before the Soviet regime collapsed) that Cubans did not need to introduce any of the reforms implemented by the USSR for its own socialist system because in Cuba "we had conceived " (that is, he had imposed since April 1986) the "Process of Rectification of Errors and Negative Tendencies", with which he sought to show the world that the socialist idea could be reformed and readapted, without self-destructing.

Even more significantly, since the end of that decade, the Cuban opposition had been expanding slowly but surely in the territory that Fidel Castro would never give up: news. Opponents used any route possible to send information abroad on constant human rights violations and the poverty of the Cuban people. Between 1990 and 2003 the first independent press agencies emerged (APIC, Habana Press, Cuba Press), a presence begins in the international press (with expanded coverage by agencies such as CubaNet, Cuba Free Press and Radio-TV Martí), there were articles and reports from the island by Raúl Rivero, Tania Quintero, Indamiro Restano, among others, to which would be added, in the second half of the nineties, new agencies such as Nueva Prensa Cubana (New Cuban Press), *Prensa Libre Oriental* (Eastern Free Press) and the Decoro (Decorum) Working Group.

In response to this complex scenario, which Fidel Castro considered too aggressive even though it was a peaceful intellectual resistance movement, in 1999 he issued Law 88 for the Protection of National Independence and the Economy of Cuba (known as the "Gagging Law"), which in its first article classed as punishable:

> "Those acts which aim to support, facilitate or collaborate with the objectives of the Helms-Burton Act, the blockade and the economic war against our people, designed to disrupt internal order, destabilise the country and liquidate the socialist state and the independence of Cuba."

This was enforced in combination with Article 91 of the Penal Code:

> "Anyone who, in the interests of a foreign state, commits an act with the purpose of harming the independence of the Cuban state or the integrity of its territory, shall be punished by ten to twenty years' imprisonment or death."

This law, with offences so broadly defined that it could be used to convict someone for any act of criticism of the government, created a new crime for the mechanism of repression: the alleged collaboration of those who criticised the government in an (also alleged) conspiracy with the historic enemy of the Revolution, United States; a "mercenary" crime which had become more dangerous to the government since the capture of the network of Cuban spies in the United States – the Red Avispa (Wasp Network) – and the diplomatic war between Cuba and the United States due to a custody battle over a little boy, Elian González Brotons (the Elian González Affair). Using this law, against the ideological background that Fidel Castro called the "Battle of Ideas", in 2003, 75 opposition journalists were jailed in the Black Spring of 2003 for the sole crime of presenting the world with a different vision to the official one.

Throughout this period, the strategy for cleaning the Revolution's face of repression and censorship internationally was the argument that all intellectual and artistic (or political) opposition was funded by the administrations of Bush senior, Bill Clinton and Bush junior, using the US Interests Section office in Havana. Although (as with other labels), it had been used before from time to time with some recognised opponents, it is from 1999 that "Mercenary of the Empire" started to become a label attached to any intellectual who declared their opposition to Cuban government policy.

_ 2003 to the present day – The fifth column
The raid on the Cuban independent press by the political police in March 2003 and the sentences issued in April, condemning the detainees to up to 27 years in prison, provoked a wave of international outrage among intellectuals of such magnitude that within the Cuban government itself, some members spoke out, expressing their concern about the negative publicity generated by such an act. They were also concerned at the number of doors closed to the Cuban Revolution's international propaganda by such obvious repression of civil liberties. It was happening precisely at a time when this propaganda had been winning many battles with the United States within international organisations, because of the strategic errors of the George Bush administration in its policy towards Cuba and the European Union's policy of condemning the Cuban government, following the line promoted by Spanish President José María Aznar (whom Fidel referred to disparagingly as El Führercillo ("The Little Hitler").

Hundreds of intellectuals, artists and politicians around the world, and hundreds of Cuban exiles, signed joint letters condemning what they began to call "The Black Spring of 2003". The arguments of those letters, along with the sheer number of internationally-renowned figures who signed them, led to a 'counter-letter' being produced by a small group of Cuban artists based on the island, members of the pro-regime UNEAC. It was entitled "Message from Havana to friends who are far away – Letter by Cuban intellectuals in response to attacks on the Revolution". The aim of this letter was obvious: the international reputation that the island had been regaining over the previous 10 years owed much to the promotional work of North American, Latin American and European left-wing intellectuals. Most of them had been excluded from the traditional circles of cultural power in their own countries and they had been literally bought by the Cuban government through invitations to the island as guests of honour, the publication or translation of their books, and even salaries and financial contributions to their personal projects in exchange for their loyalty. It is undeniable that the impact of the arrests in Cuba was so great that even many of those "loyal friends" expressed harsh criticism, such as the Portuguese Nobel Prize winner José Saramago, the German, Günter Grass (who always defended the Cuban government although, in his own country, he was a rabid critic of Communism) and the Uruguayan writer Eduardo Galeano.

The strategy of censorship and cultural repression completely changed its rhetoric: on the one hand, while the Machiavellian decision had been taken to show a more permissive face to the world, critics, political opponents and dissident intellectuals, whether Cubans on the island and in exile, or of other nationalities, began to be accused of being part of a Fifth Column against the Revolution, sponsored by US agencies and other international organisations, primarily in Europe, that the Cuban government considered enemies. On the other hand, there began a more active policy of recruiting "confused friends" from the ranks of intellectuals and artists, a strategy that would take its first steps through joint work with pro-Cuba associations, controlled by the Cuban embassies in many countries. It would eventually show its true face as an instrument for the control of culture and information when a cultural project was launched by ALBA (Bolivarian Alternative for the Americas), an alliance which, as is well known, was the brainchild of Fidel Castro and Venezuelan President Hugo Chávez. Under ALBA Cultural, as the project was known, cultural centres in every Latin American city would aim to "defend true revolutionary culture from the destructive attacks of the capitalist monopoly." It began, and maintains to this day, a sectarian policy of artistic promotion, cultural exchanges and financing of projects, conditional on loyalty to ALBA's ideological principles.

This strategy would be cleverly modified to adapt to new national and international political developments following the transfer of power from Fidel Castro to his brother Raúl in 2006. There were clearly defined and very specific adjustments made after the two big events of the "Raulist Era": the implementation of an official policy of "Change" ("Cambios" – the quotation marks obviously designed to call that term into question) that would reach all areas of the hitherto static Cuban society, and the reestablishment of relations between Cuba and the United States, after five decades of open war between the two nations.

CHAPTER II

THE CHANGES OF SKIN

REMNANTS
(1959-1971)

"We were an autonomous revolution, with an army of campesinos, who can be very good guerrillas but not necessarily good statesmen or rulers. By clinging onto so-called authenticity, we committed the errors of one-party absolutism, which is an obstacle to the exchange of ideas. It has killed dialogue and political debate – speeches come from only one side and are simply monologues."

> Reynaldo González, quoted by Juan Cruz
> El País, Madrid, 28 October 1991

In addition to these "errors of one-party absolutism", errors arising from Fidel Castro's idea that "between the two empires that plague us, it is strategically better to ally ourselves with the one that is further away, if we want to keep the independence that we have won through force of arms" as he confessed to the Commander Eloy Gutiérrez Menoyo in 1960, any analysis of changes in censorship strategy can not ignore Fidel's ideologically and politically chameleon-like personality nor his profound knowledge of the Cuban intellectual movement's role in the most important events in Cuba since its very beginnings as a nation under the colonial rule of Spain.

In those early years of the Revolution, Fidel would take an idea that Che Guevara explained in 'Man and Socialism in Cuba' in 1965: "the fault of many of our artists and intellectuals lies in their original sin: *they are not true revolutionaries*". He would add this to his personal view that the intellectuals' work effecting changes in social consciousness could undermine and thereby make it a potential enemy of anyone aspiring to control society. It was this conjunction of repressive ideas, combined with the concept of a powerful group of cultural commissars of what creative trends should be established as "revolutionary" and which had to be countered because they represented the defeated past, that formed the foundation for the three pillars of Castroist totalitarian ideology applied to the cultural world. First, the construction of the new man, a task which all Cubans, without exception, were required to take on as a personal goal; second, the production of a new analysis of Cuba's historical past that would bury definitively the remnants of Republican opprobrium (a rewriting of history that the writer Dulce María Loynaz would describe as "the invention of the derogatory term "pseudorepublic", which sought to tarnish a lustrous historical era when Cuba became the nation it is now"); and third, the gradual adoption of a Cuban version of Russian socialist realism as the "genuine creative ambit for the revolutionary epic" in the words of Mirta Aguirre, in a television interview in 1967.

Thus, there was fertile ground for the consolidation of "revolutionary" thinking on censorship: the revolutionary leaders' mistrust of the chief exponents of social thought and culture, ideological reinforcement through the increasingly close relationship with the Soviet Union, the new metropolis (despite all the difficulties in that relationship historically), the entrenchment in all spheres of national life due to the stubborn policy of belligerence towards US administrations and the "national ideological targets" for building a new Cuba according to Fidel's egocentric model. This volatile atmosphere, with its strongly bellicose reek, would invade the cultural arena, transforming it into a genuine battlefield where the creative community would try to survive with the odds clearly stacked against them because of everything that their "original sin" represented for the regime – ideologically, politically and pragmatically.

_ The 'PM' affair

As Orlando Jiménez Leal relates in his book El Caso PM: cine, poder y censura, ('The PM Affair: cinema, power and censorship'), the idea for the now legendary film 'PM' emerged in 1961, while he was working on the programme Lunes en TV ('Monday on TV'). This was just at the time when Fidel had announced a potential US invasion and declared a state of war extending across the island. The media responded to the leader's militaristic nationalism: TV stations shackled their output, with cultural programmes replaced by broadcasts of calls for unity in the face of aggression; the entire island was filled with posters warning of a holocaust if Cubans failed to fight the imperialist aggressor, and radio transmissions all assumed an identical tone of loyalty to the Revolution, in the style of the Castroist Radio Rebelde.

Jiménez Leal was sent to work on the TV Channel 2 news, as extra support to cover the Revolution's state of alert, and the director, Julio Fernández Reyes, asked him for a report on how Havana was preparing for the invasion. The result? A four-minute report showing people enjoying themselves in bars intercut with the militias preparing for combat. The director, who would have to write the script to accompany the images, told him that he would not broadcast it because it was conflictivo ("controversial"), a word the cultural commissariat applied to anything that did not conform exactly to the rigid concepts of the political bureaucracy.

It was from that first act of censorship that 'PM' was born. Believing that what had happened was natural in a state of emergency, Jiménez Leal showed the footage to his friend Sabá Cabrera Infante, and suggested turning it into a short film, "taking out all the military bits so that it wasn't a political or controversial film but rather a short ode to the night", he said, and admits that they had no intention of being provocative. They just wanted to "screen it at film clubs, at the Cinemateca, show it to friends, maybe take it to a short films festival and then broadcast it on the Lunes programme". Sabá and Jiménez Leal pitched the idea to the writer and journalist Guillermo Cabrera Infante, Sabá's brother and editor of 'Lunes de Revolución' ('Revolution Monday'), a literary supplement, who could decide what was broadcast on 'Lunes en TV'. Secure in the knowledge that the short could be shown on that programme, they started shooting.

The 'PM' broadcast was not censored: the whole country could see it on one of the major TV channels, but the censors' control apparatus was activated when it was proposed that the film be shown in Havana's cinemas. According to both filmmakers, Guillermo Cabrera Infante and others, its "unheroic" subject matter was criticised and the film itself blocked both by the Commission for the Study and Classification of Films (the censorship arm of ICAIC – Cuban Institute of Cinematographic Art and Industry) by figures who, decades later, would include a supposed defence of plurality, independence and creative freedom in their personal discourses on Cuban cinema: Alfredo Guevara, who ran ICAIC at the time; film critic Mario Rodríguez Alemán, and filmmaker Julio García Espinosa, who seemed to have forgotten about the censorship of his film 'El Mégano' six years earlier, in the days of the Batista dictatorship.

The schism that the censorship of 'PM' created in Cuban cultural circles came to the political leadership's attention. It was particularly apparent through the public condemnation of this act of censorship by over fifty important writers and artists, their signatures collected by Guillermo Cabrera Infante; the deeply critical tone (divisive according to the revolutionary creed) of the article published in 'Bohemia' magazine by Nestor Almendros, in May, and the scandal that broke out when Tomás Gutiérrez Alea (who would later become the most legendary of Cuban filmmakers and who would always remain genuinely independent creatively) daringly called Alfredo Guevara, a very close friend of Fidel Castro, an autocrat.

Such a schism would force Alfredo Guevara to propose a meeting at the Casa de las Américas cultural institution on 31 May 1961, where the censors' arguments were defeated by the strenous defence of 'PM' by most of those present. However, the next day, the Communist newspaper 'Hoy' ('Today') published the official decision to censor the short film and lied by stating that it was a majority decision by writers and artists, including the makers of the film. The filmmakers, powerless, decided to request another meeting and that is when Fidel Castro, concerned about the increasing scale of the scandal, decided to put an end to the issue by ordering a meeting with intellectuals at the National Library, using 'PM' as the starting point for a "reflection" on the artist's place in society.

At that meeting, held on three consecutive Fridays, on 16, 23 and 30 June 1961, Fidel delivered his famous speech "Words to the Intellectuals", from which the censorship apparatus would select a phrase as their battle-cry and basis for the clearly Stalinistic Cultural Policy of the Revolution: "Within the Revolution, everything; against the Revolution, no rights at all".

"What became clear after the meetings with the (revolutionary) intellectuals in Havana National Library was that the revolutionary leadership (read, Fidel Castro) sided with the faction that best suited his political interests, his desire to remain in power. He therefore supported the leaders of the former PSP [Popular Socialist Party], opting for a bureaucratic and statist path for culture, where the most critical were absorbed by the newly-created state structures (...) Thus, the Cuban politico-cultural landscape was reconfigured at the partisan whim of sovietising Castroism."
Felipe Lázaro, Cuban writer and editor.

_ The closure of 'Lunes de Revolución' cultural supplement

"'Lunes' had a huge influence on Cubans. It dealt with all the major contemporary intellectual and artistic themes, but there was a conflict between revolution and culture, and as Martí said, "culture is freedom" and a system that was going eradicate everything could not allow a vehicle talking of freedom to continue. So it had to be eliminated, and it was."
Carlos Franqui, Cuban writer and journalist in an interview with Luis de la Paz.

As can be seen, the censorship of 'PM' marked the beginning of the end for 'Lunes', a cultural supplement that, beyond the nostalgic defence and furious attacks it has provoked, essentially embodied the ideological, political and cultural contradictions of that moment in history.

First, it was founded by intellectuals with left-wing ideas but who also believed in democracy and distrusted Soviet Communism: Guillermo Cabrera Infante and Carlos Franqui; the former with the idea and the letter with his powerful position within the revolutionary press monopoly.

Second, the overwhelming majority of its staff had jubilantly clambered onto the juggernaut of the Revolution in their fight against a past they considered unjust. Their support was obvious in their first editorial, in which they announced a policy which claimed to be inclusive, but which in reality was exclusive, as it was in line with the government's political strategy to muzzle the press and culture: to be inclusive as long as that inclusivity did not affect the Revolution. That idiosyncratic and contradictory concept of inclusivity would be demonstrated in the conflicts stemming from the editorial policies of 'Lunes'. They claimed to be representatives of the new, the modern, the cultural vanguard (although researchers have all found numerous documents, letters and events showing the discontent of other young writers who were also avant-garde but who felt excluded). They were against the socialist aesthetic, which naturally gave rise to constant and savage feuds with the Communist intellectuals and Stalinist commissars entrenched in ICAIC and other centres of cultural power. They proclaimed themselves to be enemies of the old tendencies which enclosed different cultural strands within cliques of egoism and individualism. In this respect, although the writer Pablo Armando Fernández denies it, the first issues were clearly hostile towards José Lezama Lima, 'Orígenes' ('Origins') magazine and followers of that group, as well as other prominent Cuban intellectuals of the older generations who had not joined the propagandist cohorts of the Revolution.

With Cabrera Infante as editor, Pablo Armando Fernández as deputy editor and Jacques Brouté as graphic designer, who modelled the design on French cultural magazines, they produced 131 issues. Despite the internal contradictions of the project, despite their clashes with other cultural power groups, despite obvious inconsistencies in its editorial policy, despite the Mafia-like way in which it marginalised certain groups and fought against attacks and criticisms, and despite the constraints imposed on it because of its revolutionary sympathies, it has been without question the most inclusive, democratic and innovative project in the history of Cuban literature. It published works by Cuban authors of all tendencies, genres and generations; it injected new blood into the country's culture with the publication of works from the United States, the Communist countries of Eastern Europe, and the neglected literature of Asia, Africa and Latin America, by the most important writers of these regions and languages; it included the political essays of Fidel Castro, Che Guevara, Mao, Lenin and Trotsky; it disseminated the latest in European philosophy (Sartre, for example), the American beatnik movement, anti-Soviet dissidents (Pasternak being the most representative example), and writers who at the time were leading new schools of thought in other cultures; and it expanded knowledge of the arts globally through special issues dedicated to renowned Cuban, Latin American, European, and North American intellectuals and writers and to subjects of national importance such as land reform and the 26th of July Movement, and of international significance such as the racial conflicts in the United States.

The American essayist and university professor William Luis, in his essay "'Lunes de Revolución' y la revolución de 'Lunes'" ("'Lunes de Revolución' and the Revolution of 'Lunes'") (OtroLunes, No. 1, May 2007) summarises it as follows:

" 'Lunes' was published for two and a half years, from 23 March 1959 to 6 November 1961, and in that short time gained great renown and became one of the most highly-regarded literary supplements of the twentieth century. (…) The first number was only six pages long and the last sixty-four. (…) It started with a circulation of one hundred thousand copies and ended with two hundred and fifty thousand, becoming the most popular and important literary supplement in Cuban history and probably in the Western world. (…) It influenced other aspects of Cuban culture, as its staff were in charge of television scheduling, first for Channel 2, then 4, and they also hosted a weekly television programme aired on Monday nights (…) and had a record company, Sonido Erre (R Sounds), and a publishing house, Ediciones Erre (R Publications), which promoted Cuban works."

That level of influence constituted "libertinaje impermisible" ("impermissible licence") for Fidel and his cultural commissars; they sought to impose uniformity on the national creative voice, following the dictates of Soviet culture, whose most authentic artists were being crushed under the boot of "socialist realism" which would come to dominate the USSR for over 70 years and which produced barely a dozen memorable titles.

Alfredo Guevara's outrageous mistake in censoring 'PM' was used by Fidel Castro as the perfect excuse to make clear to the intellectuals his thinking on culture and the artist's place in the Revolution; thinking that would lead, in the case of films, to censorship of 'El final'' ('The end') (1964), 'Desarraigo' ('Exile') (1965) and 'Papeles son papeles' ('Paper is only paper') (1966) by Fausto Canel; 'La jaula' ('The cage'), by Sergio Giralt (1964); 'Elena', by Fernando Villaverde (1964) and 'Una pelea cubana contra los demonios' ('A Cuban fight against the demons'), by Tomás Gutiérrez Alea (1971); the withdrawal from circulation of many films whose directors had left the country: 'El bautizo' ('The baptism'), by Roberto Fandiño (1967), 'La ausencia' ('Absence') (1968) by Alberto Roldán, and 'Tránsito' ('Transit') (1964), 'Un día en el solar' ('A day in the tenement') (1965) and 'El huésped' ('The guest') (1966) by Eduardo Manet; and to erase from film history some documentaries by Sara Gómez and Nicolás Guillén Landrián, among others.

> "It was during the discussions in the National Library that it was decided to close 'Lunes' down. (...) I became absolutely convinced that Cuba was adopting a Soviet-style communist system, which I totally disagreed with (...) At the second meeting, Alfredo Guevara made extremely serious allegations about 'Lunes', saying that we were revisionists and supporters of the Poles, who at that time were the bane of the Communist countries. I asked Fidel to speak out about that, but he didn't. At that moment I realised that it was Fidel and not Guevara who was behind all this hogwash".
> Carlos Franqui, Cuban writer and journalist
> Interview with Luis de la Paz.

_ "Words to the Intellectuals": legal stamp on the censorship of
Cuban culture

It is noteworthy that in 2011, the 50th anniversary of Fidel Castro's famous
speech that became known as "Words to the Intellectuals", the new
commissars of Cuban culture (Abel Prieto, former Minister of Culture
and Miguel Barnet, president of UNEAC, head of a group of government
puppets), claimed that this ideological manifesto for censorship was still
relevant today. On 30 June 2015, 'Granma', the official newspaper of the
Communist Party of Cuba, published a statement by the writer Miguel
Barnet, reducing Cuba's cultural past to the word "horror":

> "All that changed with the Revolution. There emerged ICAIC,
> cultural centres, the amateur artists' movement and the art
> instructors, such a beautiful project (...) Today we have so many
> figures, so many great artists who would never have had the chance
> to develop, if it had not been for "Words to the Intellectuals", and
> the Comandante's idea of democratising culture and encouraging
> the search for new values in the remotest parts of the country".

Such a gross simplification of the past and present, although Manichean
and opportunistic, is useful for the current turbulent times, as it includes
only that part of the truth that suits Cuba's dictators, cultural commissars
and docile intellectuals. However, they, and most of those who defend today
the supposed validity of those words, never mention the parts of that speech
referring to the rules and limits that artists were forced to comply with if
they wanted to be accepted by the regime in a society that blindly obeyed
the orders of that regime. "Words to the Intellectuals" is a manifesto for
everything the Revolution promised and failed to fulfil in relation to culture
and its necessary freedoms, because if they had a modicum of honesty,
nobody in their right mind would praise that "relevance" after five decades of
sectarianism, exclusion, exile, prison and even executions for those who did
not abide by the rules forcibly imposed following those fateful days in June
1961.

   If they had a modicum of honesty, they would recognise that the only success of the Cultural Policy of the Revolution has been to bring culture to the masses, putting it within reach of Cubans in any corner of the island (which is not "democratisation" as asserted in Castroist political discourse, because culture in Cuba is anything but democratic and free). They would also have to accept that this policy of bringing culture to the masses was (and still is) the perfect strategy for turning culture into a government propaganda tool. In another of Fidel's speeches, in 1953, "History Will Absolve Me", regarded as the political programme of the Revolution, there is no criticism whatsoever of the culture of that society which he had taken up arms against nor any significant references to Cuban intellectuals (except to José Martí, to salute his patriotism, or to a few foreign intellectuals, praising some for their thinking which justified his thesis on the need for a revolution and attacking others for being "reactionary" and counter-revolutionaries). Moreover, none of those bearded rebels who became the ruling elite for five decades (except for an Afrodescendant, Commander Juan Almeida Bosque) believed in culture. Given these facts, and given the already demonstrated distrust of Fidel and his people towards this group because of its "original sin" (not being "true revolutionaries", as Che would say), why should we think that there is a genuine interest in culture?

However, in "Words to the Intellectuals" Fidel acknowledged that most people were not revolutionaries and set out clearly what he aimed to achieve (...the Revolution must aspire to have marching with it not only all revolutionaries, not only all revolutionary artists and intellectuals. It is possible that men and women who have a truly revolutionary attitude towards reality, do not constitute the majority of the population (...) The Revolution should only reject those who are incorrigible reactionaries, who are incorrigible counter-revolutionaries), without stating what he was prepared to do to achieve this aim of mass support.

As well as making the artist's role clear (the revolutionary (...) puts the Revolution above everything else. And the most revolutionary artist would be willing to sacrifice even his own artistic vocation for the Revolution), the greatest betrayal by the Revolution is set out here:
"Let me first say that the Revolution defends freedom, that the Revolution has brought the country a very wide range of freedoms, that the Revolution can not be an enemy of

these freedoms by its very nature; that if some are worried that the Revolution will stifle their creativity, this concern is needless, this concern is groundless".

Did the Revolution keep that promise? The answer is a resounding NO, this speech being one of the most priceless gems of Fidel Castro's customary cynicism.

_ Repression, censorship and closure of *Ediciones El Puente*

Little has been written about this other huge censorship scandal in Cuba, mostly restricted to accounts by censored writers, and it remains without question the least discussed of these episodes, as if it were forgotten that this was a milestone marking the beginning of the mass political exodus of Cuban writers. And if what happened to 'PM' and '*Lunes*' would lead to the exile of established cultural figures years later, the impact of censorship on the literary group El Puente (The Bridge), founded by the then irreverent homosexual poet José Mario Rodríguez (Havana, 1940 – Madrid, 2002), represents both the first intellectual movement in the revolutionary period and the first act of cultural repression against those young writers who, according to the stated aims of the politicians, should have been called up to join the ranks of "New Men".

But note that I wrote "irreverent homosexual poet", words that define José Mario but also point to three traits that were difficult for the revolutionary leaders to stomach: irreverent (as Fidel had already made clear the requirement to bend to his rules on the Revolution and Culture), poet (for being the bearer of original sin, not a true revolutionary) and homosexual (because softness, sensitivity and effeminacy had nothing to do with the macho ingredients of a revolution made by "those genuine representatives of Cuban manhood – our virile bearded men" as declared by the famous newscaster Violeta Casal, regarded as "the voice of *Radio Rebelde*"). In addition to these questionable qualities, the group consisted of young people from traditionally marginalised groups: blacks and women, and as a result, as the poet Belkis Cuza Malé said, they were seen as "oddballs". Moreover, they had dared to create a project which operated completely independently of the structures of cultural control established by the Revolution.

From that tumultuous 1961 to 1965, when the censor's door slammed shut on the group, Ediciones El Puente (The Bridge Publishing) took advantage of the fact that there were still independent printing presses in the country – later the government would monopolise them to concentrate publishing power in its hands. It published 38 titles (25 poetry collections, 8 books of short stories and 5 plays), and promoted the first works of, among others, its editor, José Mario (Rodríguez), Reinaldo García Ramos, Ana María Simo, Nancy Morejón, Rogelio Martínez Furé, Isel Rivero, Manuel Granados, Georgina Herrera, Gerardo Fulleda León, Lina de Feria, Nicolás Dorr, Ana Justina Cabrera, Manuel Granados, Miguel Barnet, Belkis Cuza Malé, Mariano Rodríguez Herrera, Manuel Ballagas, Joaquín G. Santana, Mercedes Cortázar, Guillermo Cuevas Carrión, Ana Garbinsky, Santiago Ruiz, Pío Serrano Silvia Barros, Évora Tamayo and the Peruvian Rodolfo Hinostroza.

Most of their testimonies (even of those who would end up becoming censors years later, such as Miguel Barnet and Nancy Morejón) point to a number of problems that such a group presented for almost all levels of the political and cultural authorities, and as a result, it was unknowingly at the centre of all attacks.

The first problem, according to many of them, was that their works were not recognised by the official institutions created by the Revolution. In the words of Isel Rivero: "Not even 'Lunes de Revolución', the 'Revolución' newspaper's weekly cultural supplement, would open its doors to us." The El Puente group made many criticisms of 'Lunes', which prided itself on (supposedly) being democratic and inclusive of all creative tendencies. It responded by becoming a powerful secret enemy of El Puente and its members.

The second problem was the decision by José Mario and those who were, along with him, the project's intellectual leaders to defend their particular modes of expression and their right to a public platform, which meant that they clashed openly and naively with the censorship apparatus, controlled since 1961 by people who sought to make all artistic creativity a single mouthpiece for propaganda.

The third problem was that, even though the persecution of homosexuals had not yet been unleashed, the obvious homosexuality of many of the group's members was already considered rather scandalous. In addition, many were black and began to make the demands which, as a marginalised race, they had been forced to silence. Their demands were included in the Revolution's programme, but they were making them "outside the channels and mechanisms" established by the revolutionary strategists, who came to accuse El Puente's black members of seeking to establish, in Cuba, something similar to the Black Power movement operating in the United States at that time. In addition, many were followers of Afro-Cuban religions and that was dangerously at variance with Fidel Castro's aim of establishing an atheistic hegemony based on the tenets of Marxist dialectical materialism.

However, José Mario and El Puente were also attacked by other groups of young writers, who were members of revolutionary institutions, such as 'El Caimán Barbudo' ('The Bearded Caiman') and 'La Gaceta de Cuba' ('The Cuba Gazette') magazines. In the latter, the author Jesús Díaz (the only one of those young cultural commissars with the good grace to publicly apologise for his political blindness) accused the project of being out of line with the revolutionary spirit of the times due to its private, selfish, hermetic and existentialist aesthetics, as well as its publication of works by exiled writers who were the subject of an order to erase them from Cuba's literary record.

The final blow came through another of those censorship strategies that would thereafter extend throughout society, including even the family: it was forbidden to maintain contact with anyone who had gone into exile or declared their opposition to the Revolution.

Fidel Castro himself put his personal stamp on the crackdown on homosexuals in a speech on 13 March 1963 (note the derogatory tone of the parts highlighted):

> "Many of these idle and alienated individuals, the children of bourgeois families, roam the streets wearing trousers that are too tight; some of them carry a guitar, try to look like Elvis Presley, and

have taken their <u>debauchery</u> to the extremes of wanting to frequent
certain public places to organise their <u>effeminate shows</u> just as the
fancy takes them. (...) There can be no place in our society for <u>such</u>
<u>degeneracy</u> (APPLAUSE.) Socialist society can not permit <u>this kind</u>
<u>of degeneracy</u>"

José Mario had flouted both bans: he was proud of his homosexuality and
became close friends with the American poet Allen Ginsberg, a world-
renowned member of the Beat Generation, a radical activist opposed to the
destructive forces of capitalism, who had been invited to Havana in 1965
by Haydée Santamaría (who at that time ran the Casa de las Américas).
Ginsberg was deported from the island soon afterwards for his statements
against the official persecution of homosexuals. José Mario was arrested,
charged with "homosexual tendencies" and sent to be reformed in the
UMAP labour camps. In February 1968, he managed to leave for Spain and
continued with his El Puente project in Madrid. In Cuba, the other members
of the group would suffer censorship for a long time.

_The Padilla Affair: the great rupture

> "What has damaged the Revolution's image to some extent
> has been the self-criticism by Heberto Padilla, Pablo Armando
> Fernández, Belkys Cuza Male, César López and Manuel Díaz
> Martínez, accusing themselves of imaginary acts of treachery,
> along with Fidel's alarming statements on culture in general
> and literature in particular in his closing speech at the Education
> Congress. All I have done is protest against these events which
> run counter to what I have always admired about the Cuban
> Revolution: showing that social justice is possible without
> disregarding the dignity of individuals, without a police or
> aesthetic dictatorship."
> Mario Vargas Llosa, *Caretas* magazine, June 1971

So many books and articles have been written about this scandal that I will just summarise it: the poet Heberto Padilla (Cuba, 1932 – Alabama, United States, 2000) was initially one of the many intellectuals who believed in the Revolution and, to serve it, he worked on the *Revolución* newspaper; he was a correspondent for *Prensa Latina* (Latin Press), the Cuban regime's press agency in the Soviet Union, from 1962 to 1964; in 1964, he was director of Cubartimpex, a company responsible for selecting foreign books for the island and, alongside his normal work with the government's publishing system and cultural press, he represented the Ministry of Foreign Trade in socialist and Scandinavian countries. However, that stay on Soviet shores allowed him to see the true face of socialism and, after he returned to Havana in 1966, he often criticised the system, especially its ideological straitjacket on culture, a straitjacket that he tried to break open through opinion pieces and articles in which he praised the work of banned authors and topics. His name, therefore, featured prominently in cultural polemics in the official publications of those years.

In 1968 he submitted 'Fuera del juego' ('Sent off the field'), a deeply critical poetry collection, for UNEAC's Julián del Casal Prize, which he managed to win thanks to the integrity of a jury consisting of Manuel Díaz Martínez, José Lezama Lima and José Zacarías Tallet (Cuban), César Calvo (Peruvian), and J. M. Cohen (British), who resisted all the pressure to stop Padilla winning the award. It should be noted that, although the repression against him received all the attention, the writer Antón Arrufat suffered similar censorship with his play 'Los siete contra Tebas' ('Seven against Thebes'), which also won the prize that year. After a long argument with the jury, UNEAC's board agreed to publish both works but included a note expressing its disagreement and stating that they were works ideologically opposed to the Cuban Revolution.

Justifiably disillusioned by this, Padilla became even more critical in his stance, and he began to show this openly in his meetings with other Cuban and foreign colleagues, never imagining that the political police was closely watching his every move. Finally, on 20 March 1971, in response to a recital he gave at UNEAC's headquarters, where he read highly critical poems

from his book '*Provocaciones*' ('Provocations'), he was arrested along with
the poet Belkis Cuza Malé, whom he had just married that year, accused of
"subversive activities" against the government. He stayed little more than a
month in prison in Villa Marista, the central prison of the political police. As
a result of the psychological torture he had received, he agreed to "star" in a
"show" in the style of the Stalinist purges against intellectuals. At a special
meeting at the Writers' Union, Padilla read his famous "self-criticism" to a
group of artists and writers that Cuban counter-intelligence had in its sights,
in which he "confessed" his mistakes regarding the glorious Revolution and
accused other colleagues present of being, like him, ungrateful intellectuals
and traitors to the great social project led by Fidel Castro.

His imprisonment and then that "confession", that the international
intelligentsia could see was clearly forced and a danger to the purity they
wrongly conferred on the Cuban revolutionary project, caused uproar in the
international press, letters condemning the revolutionary repression and
list of signatures of support for Padilla by very well-known intellectuals,
including Julio Cortázar, Simone de Beauvoir, Marguerite Duras, Carlos
Fuentes, Juan Goytisolo, Alberto Moravia, Octavio Paz, Juan Rulfo, Jean-Paul
Sartre, Susan Sontag, Mario Vargas Llosa, and many others, most of whom
definitively broke with the Revolution.

Condemned to total cultural ostracism for 8 years, Belkis managed to
leave with Ernesto (her son with Padilla) in 1979 and the following year, as a
result of international pressure and the efforts of Senator Edward Kennedy,
the poet was able to join them in New York.

Beyond the international scandal that exposed for the first time these
murky areas of censorship and cultural repression disguised as acts of
self-defence against "representatives of the decadent bourgeoisie", "those
nostalgic for the Batista past", "incapable of understanding the radical
changes that the Revolution must implement" or "softies who do not want
to share the sacrifice that the people must make in the struggle for a better
future" – labels repeated by the press – why did the Padilla Affair affect
Fidel Castro so much that he permanently deleted all those prestigious
intellectuals, artists and writers who dared to reproach him for such a

mistake from his book of future conquests (or reconquests)?

In 1998, I was at a dinner with foreign writers attending the International Book Fair in Havana, organised by writer and general Efigenio Ameijeiras, and also attended by Juan Almeida Bosque, Commander of the Revolution. I was fortunate to hear the explanation Almeida gave to a famous Spanish poet who dared to ask him about what he considered an "excessive and unaccountable act of political violence against a simple poet". It was many years ago, but I will try to reproduce what he said:

> "None of us had any political experience. Fidel was the most advanced of us, but even he didn't have any real experience, so many of those errors were due to improvising and the momentum of the epic that engulfed us all at the time. I remember Che returning from his meeting with Sartre and Simone, in 1960, very interested in an idea that the Frenchman had given him. He immediately went to tell Fidel about it. Sartre had made Che see that nobody, capitalist or socialist, had known how to harness the power of culture to transform a country's consciousness. With only a few exceptions, it was intellectuals who had joined revolutionary processes and, yet, as had happened in Russia, Stalin had distrusted them and had ended up repressing them. Sartre's idea, at least as Che understood it, was that the real mechanism for attracting artists was not to repress them, as Stalin had done, or buy them as was the case in capitalist countries. He thought that they were always a marginalised race, regarded with suspicion and eager for recognition, and therefore the most intelligent way of involving them in any process was to give them a leading role in creating strategies, setting up projects, guiding others ..., give them in a leading role in whatever you wanted to achieve.

From what Almeida said, I sensed that Fidel had gone further and wondered what would happen if he took the best of each of those three options: not repress, but control; not buy, but give them a better place in society, and not give them power in such an important area, but give certain individuals some sort of leadership role in the revolutionary struggle. It occurred to him that he could not only do it with culture in Cuba, but worldwide, with anyone who showed that they wished to help.

"With the Padilla Affair, all this turned to dust. And there's nothing that makes Fidel angrier than someone derailing a plan of his that was becoming successful," Almeida said.

Even though these ideas may have been questionable (especially because, within Cuba, such a strategy would only have been applied in certain fields and with certain figures very loyal to the regime), it is true that this was the direction that the Revolution's cultural policy began to take through institutions with an international scope, basically, the Casa de las Américas. It was during those years that the importance of cultural attachés increased in Cuban diplomatic missions with the appointment in most cases of high-profile writers and artists, or ones with important contacts outside the island. It is also well-known that Fidel admitted that Vargas Llosa was not only an enemy of the Revolution, but also a personal enemy of his. This was understandable given the now Nobel Laureate's role in the intensive campaign thanks to which hundreds of intellectuals worldwide broke off their support for the Cuban leader, regarding him as betraying the original revolutionary project. Vargas Llosa, Octavio Paz, Carlos Fuentes and others thus became the Cuban leader's personal enemies because they had shattered the vast international propaganda apparatus which, through the intelligentsia, Fidel had set up within universities, publishers, and other circles representing alternatives to capitalist culture. Until the scandal of the Padilla Affair, the Cuban social project was supported by artists and intellectuals of almost all political persuasions. After that disaster, internationally the propaganda would only have an effect on left-wing intellectuals.

In addition to that breakdown of relations, on the island itself, the Padilla Affair crushed the naivety of those who had believed in the noble aims of the Revolution's cultural policy, thus triggering the exodus (sometimes secret, sometimes public: as with all those who left from Mariel port in 1980) of hundreds of artists, writers, intellectuals and cultural professionals to the United States, Venezuela, Colombia, Panama and Spain, the major destinations of the cultural diaspora in those first decades. Those who could not or dared not emigrate chose one of three possible options: surrendering their ideas (submitting with humiliating opportunism to the principles established by Fidel's totalitarian whims); dissimulation (the majority choice) or self-isolation (the most notable cases being José Lezama Lima and Virgilio Piñera, who underwent marginalisation disguised with a few promotional opportunities, and were accused of being "elitists" and homosexuals).

All of them – opportunists, dissimulators, and self-isolators – would share the fear that reigned over all cultural circles. In 1961, during Fidel's meetings with the intellectuals at the National Library, Virgilio Pinera had raised his hand to speak and only managed to say: "I just know that I'm afraid, very afraid." I am convinced that Fidel immediately realised that fear was the most powerful weapon that could be used to make him the master and almighty lord of Cuban culture.

TRAITORS
(1971-1989)

> "... It was an awful time. (...) How could we escape from this
> atmosphere of terror that surrounded us, from bans on silly things
> like wearing bell-bottoms or having long hair, from truths held
> back for fear of being reported for ideological or moral "deviancy",
> from the reprisals for listening to music in English or to any music
> that was not Cuban made by Cubans who had not committed
> treachery, from the censure because a phrase spoken or written in
> a story or a poem sounded strange to ideological purists, from the
> torture in the prisons and the humiliation of being made to feel
> a "non-person"? It is a question that none of us has been able to
> answer convincingly".
> Carlos Victoria, Cuban writer and journalist
> Letter from the author's files.

The Cuban Revolution's credibility had suffered a severe blow with
the Padilla Affair in 1971, but that was only the beginning of a wider
phenomenon for which neither Fidel Castro's ego nor the Castroist
international propaganda structure were prepared. Hugely respected
intellectuals with high media profiles, feeling cheated by the Cuban
government, begin to poke about in the most sordid corners of the
revolutionary project; shameful zones, hidden from prying eyes under the
cloak of paradisiacal seduction with which the socialist bloc's propaganda
sought to deceive the world and win supporters for their "heroic struggle
against imperialism". Those disillusioned intellectuals would be joined by
hundreds more of all political tendencies, and all of them, the vast majority
out of conviction and some (it has to be said) encouraged and funded by
international right-wing institutions, erected a retaining wall which halted
the avalanche of lies, manipulation and obfuscation surrounding the true
situation in Cuba which had continued to pour out to the world from the
island.

The international repercussions of the Padilla Affair during the 1970s, the backlash from the international intelligentsia denouncing the revolutionary project's repression and censorship, the crushing defeat dealt to the supposed "revolutionary paradise" by the exodus of over 125,000 Cubans from Mariel port in 1980 (with the next wave of denunciations made by renowned Cuban intellectuals and artists who left the island in that mass migration, the most famous case being the writer Reinaldo Arenas), the ideological upheavals of socialism à la Soviet that made Fidel predict the fall of socialism and begin a reform process to prevent the same thing happening in Cuba, all formed the perfect conditions for a change of language in the field of censorship.

Although the term "traitor" had previously been applied to specific cases, particularly in the political sphere, from 1971 it was extended to other areas of society, especially the arts and intellectual thought. Under this new strategy, critics of the government committed treason against humanity: they betrayed Fidel, the Revolution, the Cuban people, the world's poor and marginalised, socialism, the ideals of a world free of imperialist exploitation..., etc, etc, etc. In the early years, treason of such magnitude was punishable by death but, as Commander Joseph "Papito" Serguera, one of the biggest repressors of culture in this period said, in an interview for Radio Rebelde (23 May 1972), "Our revolution in its magnanimity convicts them, but have no doubt, it will give them the opportunity to clean the stain of their betrayal and many will have the opportunity to fight on our side, once they have cleaned off this stain."

Everything seems to have started at the National Congress of Education and Culture in April 1971. The writer and critic Ambrosio Fornet tried to define the beginning of this period, calling it "El Quinquenio Gris" ("The Five Grey Years") (1971-1976), although other researchers speak of "The Grey Decade" (1971-1980) and others, including myself, prefer to extend this particular period of repression until 1989. The climate of fear as a result of Padilla's arrest, the mobilising by the extremist pro-Soviet wing of the intelligentsia, the speeches against creative freedom in various mass media such as radio, television, theatre and film by cultural commissars of all factions vying for cultural power, and the constant revolutionary propaganda about the need for the people to unite around Fidel, led artists to close ranks, resulting in the final Declaration at the Congress, which can be considered the first Censorship Manual for Cuban Culture, approved overwhelmingly and euphorically by its future victims.

Among its many other notable features, this declaration set out the methods the political commissars and ideologues of Castroism would adopt to finish the job of gagging culture. Under the declaration, all artistic work belonged to the nation, thus eliminating the right to intellectual property. Homosexual artists would not be recognised on the grounds that, due to their "disease" and "immorality", they could not be part of the artistic vanguard needed by the Revolution, giving rise to the tragic farce known as "parametración" whereby all individuals who showed "homosexual tendencies" were expelled from the cinema, radio, television, theatre and ballet. The Declaration formed the basis for a law issued shortly afterwards, "the law against indolence", in the belief that artistic creation could only be considered work if it was made available to the people and not, as had happened before 1959 (according to the commissars), if artists shut themselves in ivory towers, isolated from the people's epic. In addition, significantly, "compliance with revolutionary law" was obligatory for every artist if they were to consider themselves truly part of the people, and thus censorship and persecution of ideas contrary to those dictated by "revolutionary laws" began to form an integral part of the work of institutions and all Cubans who claimed to be revolutionary. Another highly significant development at that event was when Fidel Castro introduced to the cultural scene a tactic that had previously only been used in the political arena: blaming outside forces for some embarrassing incident or a political mistake that had tarnished the Revolution's image. He went as far as to make the absurd claim that the Padilla Affair had been conceived by the foreign media, financed by the enemies of Cuba, to create a scandal that would allow them to vilify the Revolution.

Rules on "revolutionary" culture were also drawn up by Congress. Poetry should avoid pessimism and focus on triumphant hymns to the new times. Fiction should abandon petty-bourgeois concerns and instead feature the "revolutionary and hopeful" lives of the poor, such as *campesinos*, while attacking the evils of the past such as prostitution, Batista's repression and racism. Theatre, television and film were exhorted to reflect the epic of the Revolution and the struggle to achieve the bright future described in Fidel's speeches (so it was natural that there should be censorship of the films 'Techo de vidrio' ('Glass ceiling') by Sergio Giral in 1982, and 'Hasta cierto punto' ('Up to a certain point'), by Tomás Gutiérrez Alea in 1983). Radio had to reflect Cuban music in all its variety (provided that it was made by musicians living on the island), deleting from their schedules any "foreign-sounding" music, especially music made in the "language of the enemy" – English.

The undeniable fact is that Fidel Castro and his cultural commissars, while establishing a strategy to show the world a deceptively healthy cultural face, were willing to do anything inside the island to ensure that culture did not escape their control. Here are some cases:

_ Eduardo Heras León: The other Padilla

Together with the playwright and poet Antón Arrufat, he was one of the writers most affected by the Padilla Affair. The vast majority of analyses forget that the censorship and repression he suffered occurred in the same year, 1971, and the truth is that, although Padilla would go on to pursue a successful literary career, and Arrufat would eventually produce a huge body of work, for Eduardo the experience and the fear that it instilled in him (and still does) killed off the great writer he could have been. This promise is shown precisely by the book that flung him into this hell – 'Los pasos en la hierba' ('Footsteps on the grass') – considered a classic of Cuban short story writing.

Arrufat had the good fortune to be sent to work in a library where he spent several years under close surveillance as a punishment for writing 'Los siete contra Tebas' ('Seven Against Thebes') and for being openly homosexuality. The same happened to other writers as a punishment: they were sent to "be corrected" in printing presses, book warehouses, the archives of cultural institutions or universities. Although they suffered the pressure and even humiliations of prison inmates, they were able to reintegrate themselves into society with less less trauma than Heras León, who was sent to work at a large steel plant on the outskirts of Havana: the *Vanguardia Socialista* (Socialist Vanguard) factory.

Years later, Heras León would be my literary mentor, so I was able to hear the details of his ordeal which lasted several years and which can be summarised as follows. After graduating as an artilleryman in a military school in the USSR, and having fought as one against the American invasion of Cuba in 1961, he decided to get a university degree and began to write, joining a group of friends, young artists and writers, including a still unknown folk singer called Silvio Rodríguez, and Raúl Rivero, a very young poet and today one of the most hated enemies of the Cuban dictatorship. Everyone believed firmly in the revolution, in the new era, and they began to create art in a different way: they sang of effort, of sacrifice, but they did not sugar-coat reality, they did not hide the many situations and problems happening before their eyes, nor did they lie. Therefore, both the songs of Silvio (who, as is well known, would become a propaganda icon of the dictatorship after a period of being censored) and Heras León's short stories did not fulfil the cultural commissars' requirements. In 1968, when he won UNEAC's prestigious David Prize with his book 'La guerra tuvo seis nombres' ('The war had six names'), Heras León became a target for the censors. This book, which told the story of six soldiers who fought against the US invasion in 1961, depicts, among other "sins", young men who, although willing to give their lives for the Revolution and Fidel, were afraid while they were fighting, who were flawed, critical, weak, not ideologically defined, which, according to the cultural commissars, were not the hallmarks of the revolutionary.

> "...Literature has to penetrate the deepest layers of the human being, revealing the angel and the demon which is man, uncover his innermost processes and present for everyone the only truth possible: we are imperfect and the most significant struggle is with ourselves, and we should rise above our faults, above our

mistakes, fears, resentments, anxieties (...) the only revolutionary
response was not to conceal anything: speak of courage, but
also of cowardice: speak of love but also of hate, even among
revolutionaries; speak of heroism, but also of betrayal (...) That
was the aesthetic of our generation."
Eduardo Heras León. *Quinquenio gris. Testimonio de una lealtad*
("The five grey years. Testament of loyalty").
Conference, 2007.

To this "problem" was added a greater sin: from fellow students' gossip,
censors began to suspect that Heras León had "homosexual tendencies" and
although they never managed to prove that he suffered from this "disease",
all the alarms were activated. They would ring loudly in 1970, when he won
the only mention by the Casa de las Américas Prize in the short story category
with 'Footsteps on the grass', an excellent book that starkly highlighted
the contradictions of the revolutionary epic in the ranks of the soldiers who
defended the Revolution.

The machinery of repression was set in motion, spearheaded by a
prominent censor: the writer and journalist Roberto Díaz Muñoz, then
director of *El Caimán Barbudo* magazine, where Heras León also worked.
He published an article denouncing 'Footsteps on the grass' as a counter-
revolutionary text. Shortly afterwards, the magazine published another
article where he announced the dismissal of Heras León. At the School
of Journalism where, due to lack of lecturers, Heras León gave classes in
technique and drafting, and in Latin American Literature, a meeting was
held behind the writer's back where he was accused of contaminating his
classes ideologically. The cultural press published several articles criticising
his book for being "tendentious and reactionary", and there was even a
survey on the author and the book throughout the University of Havana,
seeking support for the punishment already prepared: he was expelled
from the University, from the Communist Youth League, from his work as a
lecturer and he was deceived, being told that he would go to a steel plant as a
"trainer" in charge of the workers' education. When he arrived, the director

told him a different story, "I was told to put you to work as a labourer, straight onto the factory floor with the hot steel".

Although Heras León himself has tried to attribute the cruelty he suffered to "errors of the Revolution" and although, when someone at that time asked him why he did not leave the country, he replied, "When everyone decides to leave, there'll just be me and Fidel left", the truth is that he unjustly suffered persecution so severe that he became ill with tuberculosis, fell into depression, had suicidal thoughts (curiously, using a pistol that Fidel had given him for being outstanding in shooting exercises when he was an artilleryman), lost his marriage and, worst of all, was never again able to write with the same power as he did in earlier years, although it is impossible to deny the beauty and uniqueness of his book *Acero* ('Steel'). It is considered a classic of literature on the subject of Cuban workers, described by the Argentinian Julio Cortázar as "one of the most beautiful, poetic and humane books ever written by a Cuban." Heras León summed up this disaster as follows:

> "In literature, we are a frustrated generation. Our first books gave the promise of a substantial body of work, in both quantity and quality, but today many of us have only been able to publish a handful of books (...) We will continue writing, there's no doubt about it. Maybe we can achieve something lasting, but it will never be the same again. Our time has come and gone."

An entire book would be needed to tell the stories of the Cuban writers from different generations who were "punished" in this period. Suffice it to mention colleagues of his generation: Guillermo Rodríguez Rivera for 'El libro rojo' ('The red book'), Víctor Casaus for 'Girón en la memoria' ('Girón in my memory'), Rodrigo Moya and Renato Recio for 'En el año más largo de la historia' ('In the longest year in history'), Norberto Fuentes for 'Condenados de Condado' ('The condemned from Condado'), Jesús Díaz for 'Los años duros' ('The hard years'). Although many writers, deeply hurt and disillusioned, later went into exile, the most interesting thing is that many decided to stay and became propagandists, leaders or active exponents of the

Revolution's cultural policy, Heras León being the most notable example. Following his five-year punishment, after returning to the University to graduate in journalism and literature, he started on a slow, steady path to reintegration into the cultural world, which progressed from 1976 onwards when he was allowed to leave the steel plant and work as an editor at *Arte y Literatura* (Art and Literature), a major publishing house. That path of reintegration, which recently culminated in his winning the 2015 National Literature Prize, awarded for an author's life and work, although he has never written anything notable ever again, allows him to be considered today the intellectual who has contributed most to the development of the last four generations of writers on the island.

_ Literature behind bars

Punishment by the censors could also involve prison. The case of the writer, Reinaldo Arenas, is often discussed, and he himself would describe his time in prison in his famous book 'Before Night Falls', made into a film with a fine performance by the Spanish actor Javier Bardem. However, other great writers were also put behind bars, such as Carlos Victoria (Camagüey, 1950 – Miami, 2007, considered one of Cuba's classic short story writers) and less well-known ones such as the playwright and poet René Ariza (Havana, 1940 – San Francisco, USA, 1994) and Rafael Saumell Muñoz, writer, essayist and university professor. While Arenas was punished for his "scandalous" homosexuality, Victoria for his critical nonconformity and Ariza for his open political position, I would like to comment on the Saumell case because it serves to illustrate the absurd extremes which censorship reached in Cuba.

As he told me himself, he was sentenced to five years' imprisonment for "enemy propaganda", a crime set down in Cuba's Penal Code at Section 108.1 for Crimes against State Security.

"The strange and awful thing is that there was no such propaganda. The stories I was arrested and convicted for were never published," says Saumell. Someone reported him, the police searched his home and he was convicted because of the unpublished manuscript they found. That is not, however, the most shameful part of the affair: two renowned Cuban writers served as expert witnesses to assess whether or not to convict a young writer for a text that had not even left his home.

> "The official interrogator, First Lieutenant Braulio Maury Crespo, informed me that he had consulted two experts from UNEAC, which I was a member of, to determine whether my writing should be classified as counter-revolutionary. In one of the sessions, he showed me a piece of paper with UNEAC's logo that he then read out to me. Their verdict was overwhelming. My texts attacked the work of the revolution. When he finished reading he told me who these "collaborators" were... Adolfo Martí Fuentes and José Martínez Matos".

In the Court of Crimes against State Security, the public prosecutor asked for eight years in prison; the defence lawyer, whom Saumell had only met that day, accepted his client's guilt and simply ask for clemency, referring to his youth (he was 30), his clean criminal record and Saumell's significant contributions to various programmes on Cuban television, where he worked. The court sentenced him to the eight years requested by the prosecution. Between 1981 and 1986, Saumell, whose only crime had been to write a book, was kept in solitary confinement in the dungeons at Villa Marista, the headquarters of the Cuban political police, but was also imprisoned like a highly dangerous murderer in three maximum security prisons: La Cabaña, the Combinado del Este and Guanajay, where he was prevented from seeing his two sons, allowed a visit from his wife only every six months and where he discovered "the stark contrast between the speeches of the country's leaders and the reality of the underworld of the living and the dead in the island's prisons".

_ 1987: the year of before and after
    The formalisation of the language of censorship and repression against the freedoms of speech and the press on the island, which had begun in

1965 with the creation of the Communist Party of Cuba, was reinforced institutionally in 1975 following the First Congress of the Party, now the only political voice, and after the founding in 1976 of the Ministry of Culture, which replaced the National Commission of Culture, until that year under the Ministry of Education. A Communist intellectual close to Fidel Castro, Armando Hart Davalos, was the head of the Ministry until 1997, and although his tenure was marked by revolutionary orthodoxy and loyalty to Fidel Castro, there was better communication between the government and artists than there had been before his appointment. This included greater permissiveness which, despite its limitations, was a huge step forward when compared to the oppressive atmosphere of the first 15 years of Revolution.

In the 1980s, after the shock of the mass exodus of 1980, and with the process of institutionalisation proposed at the First Party Congress now consolidated, the cultural scene began a process of diversification that spread throughout society: the national network of art schools was extended to all regions of the country; there was expansion nationally of cultural centres acting as focal points for grassroots creativity; permits were issued for establishing cultural magazines, even in small towns; frequent events, fairs and meetings of artists were held; the publishing movement diversified and projects were launched that were unquestionably effective (beyond its political contamination) such as the National Reading Campaign, the Movement of Amateur Artists and the National Movement of Literary Workshops. Furthermore, even though they had not received the formal apologies they deserved, and although there were still many books classified as banned on Floor 15 of the National Library, many artists marginalised or "punished" during the "grey era" began to be "reintegrated".

Moreover, as the writers of the generations of the 1980s and 1990s recall, there was a golden age between 1981 and 1988 in terms of events, awards and publications that led to a creative boom and national recognition of figures from these two generations, especially in the field of literature. This did not mean that the spirit of censorship no longer reigned along with the political police's control of culture and of artists who strayed too far from permissible limits. In many cases, censorship was implemented very cleverly, hidden behind alleged errors or bureaucratic delays, while direct censors made nebulous justifications which never explained under what official criteria something was banned. As a result a new idea gained currency: censorship existed but it was impossible to say where it came from or who gave the order to censor. The finger always pointed to a ghostly figure, whose office everyone thought they knew, but no-one could accuse him of censorship.

It was, in short, a subtly suffocating atmosphere (especially in cities furthest from the more tolerant capital), which led to a gradual exodus, taking advantage of the "breath of fresh air" brought by the new cultural policy, which included, crucially, the opportunity to travel abroad for all artists who were members of UNEAC. They made use of the only service that that institution provided for years which benefited its members – acting as a travel agency and guarantor to the Cuban immigration authorities which prevented the rest of Cubans from travelling outside the island. To give you an idea of the scale of that exodus, from my generation of writers (who are now between 40 and 50 years old), of the 58 who began to be regarded "*promesas de las letras*" ("promising writers") in the early 1980s, today only seven remain on the island.

There was quite scandalous censorship in the field of visual arts, which began in 1981 and continued until the most critical year, 1987, when a large group of artists began to display thinking in their works or their performances which questioned the regime's ideology, symbols and historical leaders. This sparked repression that caused the biggest exodus of Cuban visual artists ever. In the field of literature and journalism the waters were less turbulent, and the only case of national significance occurred in Matanzas, in 1988. The writer Odette Alonso, one of the most renowned voices of my generation, describes it thus:

> "On 8 December 1988, at a poetry recital at El Pensamiento bookshop in Matanzas, Teresa Melo read "*Otros les afilan las navajas*" ("Others sharpen their knives"). The poem, iconic within Cuban poetry of the late eighties, was her catharsis after she had been held up by a mugger (...) and to try and take what

little she had, he slashed her on the head with a knife. León Estrada and another poet of her generation were with Teresa. The audience included Carilda Oliver Labra, a world-renowned poet from Matanzas, and in the front row, a mediocre poet whose name I can not remember. After listening to Teresa, he immediately asked for the floor and criticised the poem, branding it as counter-revolutionary. (...) He became locked in an open argument with the other poets, each defending their respective positions. (...) Teresa left the event and started back to Havana, just seconds before a unit of Red Berets (assault troops) burst into the bookshop, turned off the lights and, under cover of darkness, began beating and kicking those who were still there. There were several people arrested and injured, including Carilda, who was over 60 years old, who had to receive medical treatment for a severe blow to the chest. The detainees were held incommunicado for three days, underfed and subjected to frequent interrogations during which, with a huge amount of intimidation and blackmail, there were attempts to make them confess that they were counter-revolutionaries (the term "dissidents" was not in use at the time) and make them accuse the poetry recital's organisers of being their leaders. They were released without charge because there was no crime they could be accused of. (...)

"Days later, a national writers conference was held in Santiago. There were activities at various venues, including the *Teatro Guiñol Santiago* (Santiago Puppet Theatre) (...) León and I were there one morning, sitting in the last row, when Jorge Luis Hernández and José Manuel Fernández Pequeño read out UNEAC's official statement on the incident, which had come about because Teresa had complained to Abel Prieto, its then president, and he had launched an investigation. Mustering his courage, León said publicly that the statement's account of the incident was inaccurate and incomplete. They immediately made him get up onto the stage, and under the spotlight, like a folk singer without a guitar, he gave the details (…) The outrage was immediate and widespread. That night at UNEAC's provincial headquarters we signed a declaration drafted by the conference organisers in an unprecedented act of courage and dignity – few in Cuba dared to lay themselves on the line in that way. The statement condemned the attack and demanded a thorough investigation with its findings to be acted upon".

_ PAIDEIA Group – Third Option

In this environment in Cuba influenced by *perestroika* and *glasnost*, the PAIDEIA project also managed to emerge (if not survive). Without being a group or movement, it had an impact on the ossified official cultural scene of the second half of the 1980s. Again, like El Puente, it aimed to provide a space for promoting the island's abundant and varied avant-garde arts, in all their forms, independent of the power structures set up by the Ministry of Culture, such as UNEAC and the Hermanos Saíz Association.

The only real contact with officialdom was the Group's chosen venue in Old Havana, the result of discussions with the Alejo Carpentier Centre. In the living room of Carpentier's house on Empedrado Street, there were literary, artistic and musical activities with writers such as Marilyn Bobes, Omar Pérez, Victor Fowler, Antonio José Ponte, Emilio García Montiel and Ernesto Hernández Busto, usually led by Reina María Rodríguez; painters of the stature of Flavio Garciandía, Arturo Cuenca and José Bedia (at the time when their careers were just beginning to take off); musicians like Carlos and Víctor Varela, and choreographers like Marianela Boán, founder of one of the legends of Cuban dance, the *Danza Abierta* (Open Dance) group. After each activity the space would be opened up for public debate, and often critics would take part whose work would become very well-known, such as Gerardo Mosquera, Desiderio Navarro and Iván de la Nuez.

This project presented an alternative for promoting artists born in the 1950s and 1960s whose path to official promotion schemes had been barred, basically because they were avant-garde. Unquestionably, its aim was to achieve an alternative cultural policy to that of the cultural institutions, and the brief but well thought-out framework of ideas published in the 'Naranja Dulce' ('Sweet Orange') bulletin were scandalously distant from the ideological principles that the regime had conceived for culture. Nonetheless, the project aimed to dynamite the status quo from within, proposing a dialogue that would transform the "Sovietisation" which was the basis of "revolutionary" cultural policy. However, not even this attempt to establish channels of communication over this official policy, and not even the fact that many parts of their public statements, theses and other documents defended socialism (its "Declaration of Principles" of 1990 repeated the slogans of the official rhetoric: "…Socialism or Death. The Homeland or Death. We shall triumph"), not even their political views which to some extent followed the party line, were enough to allay the cultural commissars' concerns about the subversive nature of the project from its very inception in 1989, and they began to act both openly and secretly to put a stop to it. And so, almost from its conception until its demise in 1992, PAIDEIA (and the *Movimiento Independiente de Opinión Tercera Opción* (Third Option Independent Opinion Movement) which was formed out of this project) had to fight battles of clarification at every step, never imagining that, because of the essence of what they were proposing, nothing would be any use against the totalitarian state that they were naively trying to change.

As can be seen, these were underground tremors, not because they were less significant, but because the well-oiled machinery of repression buried them and prevented their shockwaves from having an impact on the cultural scene and, it is also fair to say, because the repressors and censors had become so expert in their methods that they rarely committed mistakes such as those perpetrated against the visual artists or the above incident, which began to be called "the kicking of Carilda" in literary circles.

To all these tremors must be added a factor discussed earlier: the influence on Cuban cultural thinking of news and publications about the changes wrought by *perestroika* in the Soviet Union and the ideological conflicts and intense debates provoked by *glasnost*. Against this background, two events in 1987 would shake another group, Cuban journalists: the Sandra Case and the naive rebellion by journalism students.

_ The Sandra Case
Issue 93-94 of the magazine 'Somos Jóvenes' ('We are young') of September 1987, shook the whole of Havana. An article, ('El caso Sandra') ('The Sandra case'), by journalist and author Luis Manuel García Méndez, as he explained: "Recounted the adventures and misadventures of a hooker (before they had entered national folklore). At that time, they only had a life in police reports, like fictional characters. Their baptism certificate came much later when He [Fidel Castro] personally boasted that in Cuba we had the most cultured prostitutes in the world".

It was so rare for such an article to escape the censors' control that there were contradictory reactions. On the one hand, some stated that the journalist had been arrested, the magazine had been closed down, the unsold copies had been retrieved, the political police were hunting down the copies that had been sold, and that the editor had been sacked. On the other hand, it was said that the Party had had a hand in the article, that Fidel Castro himself had approved it, that its publication was part of a strategy for implementing a kind of *perestroika* in Cuban journalism and that Luis Manuel would not have written something like that if he were not part of the "apparatus" (a political police agent). The truth is that each of those copies sold (200,000 according to Luis Manuel) were like gold dust on the black market and the article provoked a heated debate among journalists throughout the island, confused by the succession of "changes" in Cuba since 1986. This was at a time when Fidel Castro, in a speech in which he acknowledged that everything done up to then had been a disaster, a series of mistakes, had launched a review of his own policies, determined to show that socialism could be renewed without being damaged. Cubans would never forget a phrase in that speech, "Now let's build socialism", which made most wonder, "So what have we been doing for the last two decades?" In journalism, this "fresh air" introduced terms like "openness to a critical and militant journalism", "greater commitment to the exercise of judgement", "the need for investigative journalism and opinion to better analyse reality", all part of a supposed but never applied "New Information Policy".

Luis Manuel has explained that he wrote the article in line with the government's proposal on how to dealing with problems. "It's much better to wash our dirty linen in public before we get buried in dirt," Fidel Castro had said at the Second Plenary Session of the Communist Party's Central Committee, where he also stated that it was wrong to continue hiding mistakes "for fear that the enemy finds out over there in Miami". However, in 'El Caso del Caso Sandra' ('The Case of the Sandra Case') ('Habaneceres' blog, 1 January 2007) the journalist recognises that "Later we would realise that the phrase was just a handful of words joined together by the laws of syntax, and only referred to linen previously identified by the prêt-à-porter of power".

The consequences for the "protagonists" followed the tepid course of the new policy of repression and censorship: subtlety and cunning. Luis Manuel was not arrested, but was sentenced to "write about distant planets, curiosities and ancient history. Any post-Renaissance event was considered highly topical and they were not confident that I could tackle it with due prudence". The editorship of the magazine was handed over to a mediocre amanuensis and 'Somos Jóvenes', which for a few months had captured the attention of thousands of readers interested in real issues, reverted to the rag full of nonsense and platitudes which it had once been, more suited to the censors.

As usual, this policy began after a meeting with the Grand Censor, Carlos Aldana, a man who had Fidel's total confidence, who would eventually be sacked from his position of enormous power for corruption. However, the most interesting discovery from that moment for Luis Manuel and his colleagues (who all, except for one journalist, defended the article) is precisely the lesson that that act of censorship bequeathed to the history of Cuban journalism:

> "As we later learned, Carlos Aldana was the conduit for Fidel Castro's anger, who was enraged after reading those unplanned

rags. (...) After those events, we realised that the journalism
we had attempted for a few months could be desirable for the
system imagined by Karl Marx during his afternoons at the British
Library, or for the libertarian, democratic socialism that Cubans
deserved. However, the farm which was Cuba could not allow a few
busybodies to question the judgment of overseers, foremen, farm
managers, still less the landowner. A farm just needs a propaganda
tool, an amplifier of pre-packaged ideas to fulfil a purely didactic
function".

_ The naive rebellion of journalism students

As some of us who experienced this momentous event at first hand have
said, although there had already been other controversial meetings between
university students and Fidel Castro (in the 1970s at the *Universidad de Oriente*
(Eastern University) and in the mid-1980s at the University of Havana, as
I recall), our 14-hour meeting with an arrogant Supreme Leader, angry at
our lack of respect, was never reported in the Cuban press despite being
the greatest act of rebellion by journalists against the Castroist propaganda
establishment.

The meeting was held on 26 October 1987 in a theatre in the Palace of
the Revolution. Its objective? The students from the Faculty of Journalism
at the University of Havana had demanded a discussion at the highest level
on the role of the press, our responsibility and on the freedoms we felt had
been restricted. It was a response to the great confusion that reigned over
Cuban journalism, with leaders and professors unable to answer a single
one of our questions about the limitations which shackled our profession
and condemned it to mediocrity. In line with a slogan Fidel Castro used in
one of his speeches, we wanted to establish a "sincere dialogue between
revolutionaries". From the outset, some began to express their annoyance
at the conditions imposed for that meeting: it was not an open meeting as
many of us had gullibly imagined (it was held in private and by invitation)
and, as well as our Faculty professors, all the directors of the national media

were invited. Despite this, a suggestion of ours was never taken up: the publication of what was discussed, to serve as a manual for the rest of our colleagues on the island and all those Cubans who wanted to contribute to the topic under discussion.

I remember exactly the circumstances that led to it all. The cultural press was now publishing articles (still timid, but enlightening) on the changes in the freedoms of press and opinion in the Soviet Union. Censorship had began to focus on magazines such as 'Moscow News' and 'Sputnik' (finally banned in 1989), because of the dangerous image projected by many of their articles on the "Revolution within the Revolution" that perestroika represented for Soviet socialism. Some of the students objected to the obsolete and politicised curriculum for journalism, which became a daily topic. If that were not enough, the Faculty of Journalism had been the first at the University of Havana to refuse to comply with the bureaucratic farce, dictated by the cultural policy of the Revolution, that "all Cuban institutions must be declared Cultural Modules", which meant that amateur groups had to be set up, a contrived idea which failed to interest any of the journalists, even though many of them (like me) had links with the arts. A wind of dissent was blowing through the Faculty. We debated everything that affected our training and our performance as journalists and this was taken up by the leaders of the Federation of University Students (FEU), by the professors and by the university management, in what I believe a worthy act (many say the only one) by Lázara Peñones, the Dean, who, despite her bad reputation as a conservative and censor, decided to support us.

The real organisers of the whole process were Lidia Señarís Cejas (FEU president), Ana Laura Bode, Jorge Fernández Era, and Alexis Triana, then FEU's Culture Officer, an intelligent journalist who, through fear and subsequent threats, was converted into a sad functionary in the service of the government propaganda machine. Although Lidia Señarís was part of my group, it was Alexis whom I saw for weeks on end in conversations with many of us who, in the classroom, in the corridors, and even outside the Faculty, criticised certain aspects of the schematic, closed and bureaucratic framework imposed on journalism on the island. "You, as a young writer, can contribute a lot," he told me one of those days, when he found out from a mutual friend that I had managed to get samples of the American New Journalism from the libraries of important writers I knew. I was reading and then passing them on to trusted fellow students, convinced that the theory of journalism à la russe (which formed the basis of our curriculum) could do nothing to make us the great journalists we dreamed of being.

Therefore, most of us discussing these issues warmly welcomed the proposal by the Faculty management, professors and FEU leaders, for each class to draw up a questionnaire, which we would present to the highest state authorities on journalism. Most important was the deeply democratic process in the drafting of those questions. Each class (there were five in all, one per year) met and devised their questions. Then, at a small meeting to which everyone was invited, but only the most interested attended, Lidia Señarís read out each question in turn, repeated questions were combined into one, and there was a vote on each question that should be included in the questionnaire, out of 96.

We asked about almost all of the factors which, in our opinion, would gag us when we graduated: the triumphalism in the news, the lack of criticism, the leaders' contempt for journalists, the ideological Manichaeism, the lack of freedom of information, the rigid channels for the approval of work, the internal control structures for information which we considered mechanisms for censorship. We even raised highly topical issues such as the news treatment of the crisis in socialism, the transparency we believed was needed in the process for correcting errors in the media, a better information policy on Cuba's involvement in international conflicts, and even Fidel Castro's personality cult, the signs of which were already beginning to worry us.

After sending the questionnaire to the Grand Censor's offices, the DOR (Department of Revolutionary Orientation) of the Party's Central Committee, we received a reply shortly afterwards, from the man himself, Carlos Aldana. And so it happened – we were taken to the Palace of the Revolution Party theatre and, once we were seated, the curtain rose and there, sitting with student and government leaders, was Aldana, arrogant and all-powerful.

There was an introduction by Lidia Señarís who, as FEU President, told Aldana that, with all the frankness of our youth, we were there to talk to whoever could clear up our doubts. There then began a round of questions which the Censor answered with empty verbiage and an obvious contempt for our opinions. Our discontent could be smelt in the air, and we expressed it even more in the recess that Aldana himself proposed. One of our professors, the journalist Wilfredo Cancio, recalls:

"When the debate resumed, Castro appeared on the platform, explaining that someone from his advisory team had informed him of an interesting student meeting and he had decided to spend some time there out of curiosity. In the heat of the discussions in the hours that followed, when an angry Castro accurately referred to speeches in the first session, we realised it was a blatant lie: the man who now spoke to us in patronising and dogmatic tones had full knowledge of the minutest details of that official ambush, and had even followed everything that had happened before his arrival on closed circuit television.

"(...) Defiant words from a student who asked Fidel to let him speak, and ''not to interrupt like a father who doesn't want to listen to his children,'' made the dictator fly off the handle in a way that none of us present could ever have imagined. Castro banged on the table and said he would let him speak, but threatened to withdraw from the meeting if he was not allowed to make certain key points.

"Another student referred to an alleged headline by 'Granma' newspaper which gave Castro the credit for the donation of a sugar mill to a Central American country. We never knew he managed it, but in less than a minute an assistant appeared on the stage with the page containing the headline to correct the mistake: "Cuba donates sugar mill to Nicaragua''. A hardened party activist tried to lighten the tense atmosphere with a phrase which was in fact a real slap in the face for Castro, "Gentlemen, we're treating Fidel as if he were Kim Il Sung and he's not the same''.

"It was all too much for a man accustomed to the comfortable phrases of his entourage. I can still remember the unease on Aldana's face and the obvious anger of Castro's personal assistant, Doctor José "Chomy" Millar, the nervousness of other leaders on the panel and the uncertainty that gripped almost everyone, as well as the tears of several students who came up to me in one of the breaks, with no words to express the profound disillusionment they felt. That was the day when many young people stopped believing for ever.

"The climax came with a question by Amir Valle, now a writer who has taken the path to exile in Germany, who tried to rescue the night from a monumental fiasco with a reasonable suggestion, "Comrades, it would be unforgivable if we lost this opportunity for Fidel to tell us what he thinks of *perestroika* and the changes in the Soviet Union". Castro took the microphone to bring that unfortunate night to a close and, as has been usual since 1959 in meetings with his presence, to exercise his right to the last word."

What followed was terrible. A commission from the Opinion of the People Team (the body whose responsibilities include informing Fidel Castro of any critical public opinion) ambushed us the next day, asking us all our opinion on what had begun to be described as "unpardonable disrespect to the *Comandante*". Carlos Aldana, now even more cynical and repressive, decided to hold a meeting with every journalism class to answer the questions that had not been answered (the majority) and those meetings were pure indoctrination and pure threat. Fidel Castro, in a rage during a Party meeting, called reporters who questioned him *mojonetes* ('stupid shits'). The political police met with the "most recalcitrant" and embarked on a policy of fear and unbearable betrayal. The Young Communist League and the Communist Party launched a campaign of score-settling and punishments which they continued even after many of us had graduated. Strangely, these purges spread to the other faculties of the University of Havana. Our repressors decided that what had happened showed that we needed contact with reality and that was how the days of work in construction or agriculture became mandatory. All I can say is that the atmosphere in my fourth and fifth years as a student was quite simply foul.

The outcome? First, many were sent to perform social service in remote regions of the island. Just as an example, one of the leaders, Lidia Señarís, was punished and, upon graduation, was sent to work in the mountains of Guantánamo. I was sent to Cienfuegos, despite having an excellent job offer for the Middle East Department, my specialism, at Prensa Latina press agency, in Havana. Some would abandon journalism altogether. Exile would be the final destination of many others. A significant number (although none who had had a leading role in the student rebellion) would, with nauseating opportunism, take up jobs implementing the new censorship, repression and mutilation of press freedoms imposed nationwide after October 1987. They are still there, even to this day, and it is they who are responsible for the mediocrity, analytical vacuum, triumphalism, shameful deceitfulness and gross sloganeering of the Cuban journalism of today.

MERCENARIES
(1990 – 2003)

The atmosphere around Cuban culture tensed dramatically at the beginning of this period, as it became entrenched in the "*plaza sitiada*" ("state of siege") mentality that stifled much public artistic expression, but not creativity itself, which exploded. It would gradually emerge from that period of stagnation at the end of the 1990s, to show a clear recovery in the early twenty-first century.

In economics, there was a total crisis (euphemistically called a "Special Period" by Fidel Castro). This seriously affected the state subsidy to culture and, among many other restrictions, triggered the biggest contraction in publishing in the history of the Revolution. Many periodicals ceased to exist or drastically reduced their pages, and publishers produced short runs of the few books that were actually published, with the "plaquette" system imposed on the whole island (loose sheets with poems, short stories or fragments of novels, with which writers had to be satisfied).

In the field of social thought, the country was shaken by debates (never in official forums) on Francis Fukuyama's theory on the end of history. It seemed to have a lot of substance, not only when analysing the fall of socialism and the increasing triumph of liberal thought throughout the globe, but also when considering all the "*caídas*" ("defeats" for which read "forced changes") that the changing international situation dealt time and again to the hitherto unshakable economic, political and ideological structure of the Revolution. Within this, the only immovable element was the obstinacy of Fidel Castro who, even with his skill as a political chameleon, was unable to conceal the arm-twistings he was forced to accept.

In ideology, the government propaganda of the "last bastion of socialism" was reinforced by a sustained national and international campaign stating that the sacrifice of Cubans was the key to the salvation of a world already entirely dominated by the most reactionary forces of capitalism. At the end of this period there was another burst of propagandistic fanaticism, known as the "Battle of Ideas", a change of skin in the strategy of the fight against imperialism that Fidel Castro would implement by taking advantage of two events in 1998 and 1999: the detection and trial in the United States of the *Red Avispa* (Wasp Network), 27 Cuban spies who had infiltrated key government agencies, the army and the secret services, in what is the biggest defeat of the Cuban intelligence services to the present day; and the diplomatic and propaganda war for a Miami family to return Elián González Brotons, a small boy whose mother had taken him from Cuba on a raft without his father's permission. Interestingly, Fidel Castro himself, in the light of government surveys which showed that the Cuban people no longer believed in the much-heralded US invasion, was forced to recognise that it was time to put the theory aside. However, as he was not ready to take off his uniform of a warrior against the empire, in his closing speech at the seventh Congress of the Young Communist League on 10 December 1998, he disguised his defeat thus, "The dangers of military aggression can not be ruled out entirely, but today, today this is what is important: the battle is a battle of ideas".

Terrain so eroded, with such seismic shifts, gave unusual prominence to the Cuban opposition intelligentsia, forcing the censors and cultural repressors to refine their strategy. They sought to discredit, both nationally and internationally, the claims made by intellectuals and artists who openly opposed the government, to reduce the impact of their statements which were indisputable. They therefore transferred from political discourse to official intellectual discourse a term hitherto used almost exclusively for the government's political opponents – "mercenaries" with the addition "of the empire" because it coincided with the derogatory terminology used in open forums, current affairs debates on television and other ideological campaigns forming the Battle of Ideas.

For the first time in five decades, the process of eliminating the intellectual as a figure contributing to political debate, generating ideas and shaping a nation's social thought, was finally reversed. After several generations of Cuban artists, writers and professionals had lost their voice and had been condemned to cede that space to politicians and their most loyal cultural commissars, they would recover it, even if that recovery has been very slow to the present day.

Let us examine examples of this "opposition" intellectual leadership through the most outrageous acts of censorship in this period:

_ May 1991: The "Letter of the Ten"

I had now completed two years of social service working as a journalist at Radio Ciudad del Mar (Sea City Radio) in Cienfuegos and was an active member of UNEAC's Writers Association in the province, when its local president, Orlando Garcia, a serious historian, with whom since then I have shared a brotherhood of mutual respect. "Do you think we should sign this?" he said and handed me a piece of paper. I read it. It was a pronouncement by UNEAC's National Council harshly criticising 10 colleagues who had sent a "treacherous" declaration demanding a set of changes that, according to the text I read, reproduced the demands with which the enemies of the Revolution sought to destroy Cuba. "What about these people's declaration?" I wanted to know, because it seemed absurd to request a signature condemning someone or something without explaining clearly what "treason" it was we should condemn. As a condition for signing, we agreed to officially request the original letter and also to be informed of the opinions of those 10 colleagues and what had led them to draft what was already being called "La Carta de los Diez" ("The Letter of the Ten" – the original text of which we saw just days later). In all honesty, none of UNEAC's members in Cienfuegos wanted to sign in support of the sinister and manipulative pronouncement of the national leadership. I heard that something similar had happened in some other provinces, and I also know that many who did not attend meetings or respond to calls to sign were included on the lists, as the president of UNEAC himself, Abel Prieto, had said that in extreme cases such as these "silence or absence means consent". I mention this in fairness to those who opposed one of the cultural commissars' dirtiest tricks against colleagues whom they knew perfectly. Manuel Díaz Martínez, an essential figure in Cuban poetry (and one of those "mercenaries"), recalls:

> "There were few Cuban intellectuals who resisted official pressure
> and refused to sign that document, which contained such serious
> and, ultimately, false charges that were never proven. Among those

who refused, I recall the poet and essayist Fina García Marruz, the poets César López and Emilio de Armas, the historian Manuel Moreno Fraginals and the authors Reynaldo González and Alberto Batista Reyes, who was summarily dismissed from his post as director of the *Editorial Letras Cubanas* publishing house". ("La carta de los Diez" ("The Letter of the Ten"). Encuentro de la Cultura Cubana. No. 2, 1996. p. 22.).

What had incurred the oppressors' wrath? That ten artists, most of them significant figures, had dared to question the way that Fidel Castro was managing his property, the farm estate called "Cuba". They were asking for changes which in other countries would not even occupy the newspapers' filler pages, but which in Cuba the dictatorship considered "enemy maneouvres". The requests in "The Letter of the Ten" included asking the government to foster civic dialogue, in which all political tendencies in the country were represented, in order to find a Cuban solution to the Cuban crisis; the election of deputies to the National Assembly through direct and secret ballots of citizens; the immediate release of political prisoners; removal of the restrictions preventing Cuban citizens from leaving and returning to the country; and the re-establishment of campesino free markets (summarily eliminated by Fidel Castro years before) to stimulate agricultural production and reduce food shortages.

Ten names would be crucified this time by the machinery of repression: the writers María Elena Cruz Varela, Raúl Rivero, Manuel Díaz Martínez, José Lorenzo Fuentes, Bernardo Marquéz Ravelo, Manuel Granados, Roberto Luque Escalona and Nancy Estrada Galván (the first six renowned Cuban literary figures), the journalists Fernando Velázquez Medina and Víctor Manuel Serpa. Shortly afterwards, the translator from German, Jorge Pomar, actor and singer Alberto Pujol Parlá and filmmaker Ricardo Vega would also add their signatures.

Fidel Castro regarded the way the letter was disseminated as clear provocation: copies were sent to the Council of State and the Central Committee of the Communist Party, but also (in the knowledge that the

Cuban press would never publish the original letter) to foreign newspapers, basically in the United States and Europe. As usually happens in such cases, to counteract the effect of the propaganda in the foreign press, which began to publish the demands, tame national journalists began a shameful smear campaign against the signatories. The first editorial, published in 'Granma' newspaper, the mouthpiece of the Communist Party, had the crude headline "A new maneouvre by the CIA" and, using the classical rhetoric of "collaboration", "treason", "annexationism", announced that, according to the repressors, it was the United States' new tactic against Cuba – the use of mercenaries. Even more cynically, there were attempts to discredit the signatories personally and professionally, and so, among other lies, Maria Elena was "a minor poet" (although everyone knew that she was already a great writer), Raúl Rivero and Manuel Díaz Martínez were saddled with the label of "filthy drunks and poets without any works to their name", and in general, all were accused of wanting to gain international prestige through a scandal, with the obvious profits that they would gain (in addition to what their capitalist "masters" had already allegedly paid them for their mercenary work).

The international outcry in response to these abuses was almost as great as it had been with the Padilla Affair. On 31 May 1991, Miami's El Nuevo Herald newspaper published a statement of condemnation, signed by leading figures of the Cuban intelligentsia in exile and foreign intellectuals, including Mario Vargas Llosa, Oscar Arias, François Revel, Susan Sontag, Hugh Thomas, Jorge Semprún, Fernando Savater, Fernando Sánchez Dragó, Gastón Baquero, Carlos Alberto Montaner and Heberto Padilla.

That outcry made the tyrant even angrier. As well as the "acts of repudiation" with which they were persecuted in their homes and workplaces, as well as the "visits" by political police officers suggesting that they distance themselves from a "manoeuvre against Cuba that the CIA is using you for" (as one said to Jorge Pomar), and as well as the dreadful public humiliation, mass beatings and physical injuries received by several of them (María Elena Cruz Varela and Jorge Pomar being the worst affected), all doors were closed to the signatories and to others who added their signatures to the letter or supported it. Any who were members of UNEAC were asked to recant or be expelled (none agreed to renounce their ideas and they were therefore subjected to "dishonourable expulsion"); journalists were also expelled, from UPEC (Cuba Union of Journalists); most had their employment contracts terminated (Nancy Estrada Galbán, for example, was sacked from 'Mujeres' ('Women') magazine, where she was editor, Díaz Martínez was fired from the radio station where he was culture correspondent, and Pomar was dismissed from his post as head of the translation department at the publishing house Arte y Literatura). Some of them were even sentenced to prison on charges of "defamation" and "enemy propaganda", such as Jorge Pomar, María Elena Cruz Varela, Fernando Velázquez Medina, and Roberto Luque Escalona.

The harassment, the unjust prison sentences, the daily repression and the closing down of all possibilities for personal and professional fulfilment obliged all the signatories to emigrate. The only exception was the poet and journalist Raúl Rivero and he would finally emigrate just over a decade later, forced by other, but also repressive, circumstances.

As a postscript, I will add that perhaps this atmosphere intensified the repression used by the political police to destroy an interesting artistic project which had emerged in Cienfuegos that same year, the Extropista Movement, an opposition group led by Arturo González Dorado, a very young writer, along with other friends of his generation. It was a project which, after individuals were repressed one by one, caused the expulsion of González Dorado from the University. There would also be severe repression of other intellectuals who were considered "lone wolves" of Cuban literature. Specifically in Cienfuegos, I must mention the case of the author Armando de Armas who had to flee the island in a boat, an escape that could be used as a script for a Hollywood movie.

_ July 1991: 'Alice in Wondertown'
In this period the cinema censors also gagged 'Un día de noviembre' ('A November day'), by Humberto Solás (1992) and 'Cerrado por reformas' ('Closed for Renovations'), by Orlando Rojas (1995), the shooting of which was

suspended on the third day because it was considered counter-revolutionary. However, it was '*Alicia en el pueblo de Maravillas*' ('Alice in Wondertown') by Daniel Díaz Torres (1991) which became a national scandal because of the Kafkaesque nature of the censorship it suffered.

With a script by Daniel Díaz Torres and the Nos-y-Otros Group (essentially the writer Eduardo del Llano), filming of 'Alice in Wondertown' began at the time of greatest upheaval before the fall of communism, in 1989. It had a glittering cast – Thais Valdés, Reynaldo Miravalles, Alberto Pujols, Carlos Cruz, Raúl Pomares, Alina Rodríguez, Jorge Martínez, and Enrique Molina. Before its premiere in Cuba, on 13 July 1991 in the Charles Chaplin Theatre in Havana, it had already been shown that February in Germany at the Berlinale, one of the most prestigious international film festivals, where it received a special mention by the jury.

As I have said, it had been filmed at a time when the official discourse had led people to believe that they could talk about anything, but the film came to be screened in a very sensitive, ideologically complex period – the year when socialism was breathing its last, plunging the country into a deep economic depression, especially for culture. Furthermore, 'Alice' had received a lot of exposure in the Cuban press and cultural media, as it somehow represented the triumph of creativity over the vicissitudes of the economy. Ever since that early publicity, there had been comments that it was a critical film, which meant that it was gaining a "bad reputation". As a result, on 17 July, just three days after its release, all copies were withdrawn from the island's theatres.

> What did the censors see in the film that could be detrimental to the Revolution?
> Eduardo del Llano ("*La maravillosa historia de 'Alicia' contada por Eduardo del Llano*" ("The wonderful story of 'Alice' told by Eduardo del Llano.") in '*El cine es cortar*', blog by filmmaker Manuel Iglesias, 2001) recalls:
> "The truth is we wrote what we wanted to write, without imposing restrictions on ourselves. If there is no more in the film, it is because we did not want there to be more. We liked the idea of a

spirited and idealistic girl, recently graduated, arriving at *Maravillas de Novera* [Wonders of Novera] (an anagram of *"Averno"* [Hell], ha) a small town where everyone is guilty. A place where everything is bad, but nobody says so. It seemed a bold and fun thing to do, because we were doing it from the inside."

However, most significantly, many key parts of the plot raised questions about all kinds of hegemony within a society; not only the monopolies of traditional power such as the Catholic Church, bureaucracy or the economy, but also all kinds of control of the masses (and here it clearly targeted the Revolution, although it did so with the satirical tone inherited from the best Cuban cinema of the early decades of the revolutionary period, *'Las doce sillas'* ('The twelve chairs'), 1962; *'La muerte de un burócrata'*, ('The death of a bureaucrat'), 1966, and *'Los sobrevivientes'* ('The survivors'), 1979, all by Tomás Gutiérrez Alea.

Analysing what happened, according to Del Llano and Díaz Torres, such an absurd reaction by the censors may have been due to a combination of factors. First, the covert repression of the intellectual and cultural scene since the beginning of 1991, as the authorities could not forget that the disintegration of socialism had begun precisely because of criticism by some reformers and intellectuals' hard work undermining it. Second, the public comments on the film's critical messages based on several incomplete copies circulating clandestinely in Havana. Third, the praise 'Alice' received at its screening at the Berlinale in Germany, which generated comments in the press and in the European film world, amazed that such a film would be allowed in Cuba, the only socialist dictatorship with any life. Fourth, the regime's tantrum over the protests by several filmmakers against government plans to merge ICAIC with Cuban Television and the film department of the Revolutionary Armed Forces in order to save money. However, the filmmakers saw it as a mechanism for monopoly control because, if this merger went ahead, it would all be under military management.

Del Llano recalls, "The newspapers really had a go at us. *Granma*,

Juventud Rebelde, Trabajadores, Tribuna, Bohemia, published articles with titles such as *"La suspicacia del rebaño"* ("The suspicion of the flock") and *"Alicia: un festín para los rajados"* ("Alice: a feast for the swine"), in which they called us counter-revolutionaries and slackers", and says that although the the the scriptwriters wrote a letter to the Central Committee they never received a reply, "We could not reply. We could not debate."

What marked a change in direction for censorship policy was that this censorship was only targeted at the film, in an attempt to deaden its social impact, although this, as usual, turned it into a cult object for the underground video market on the island. However, there was no severe crackdown on the "sinners", as Del Llano recognises. "Although there were low level attacks on us, and rumours, and for a while we were waiting for our imminent conversion into Wondertown characters, into eternal failures, it's fair to say that neither the actors nor Daniel, nor I, who was then a professor at the Faculty of Arts and Literature, had work or social problems as a result of 'Alice'..." Del Llano however forgets the filmmaker Julio García Espinosa, then director of ICAIC, who was replaced by Alfredo Guevara, the Pope of censorship of Cuban cinema since his leading role against the short film, 'PM'.

I was still in Cienfuegos, working as a radio reporter, when the director, Armando Sáez, a grey journalist with a censor's soul, called a meeting and instructed us to attend the screening of the film at the city's biggest cinema with these words, "It's a counter-revolutionary work, but the Party leadership has decided to show that we are not at all afraid of such provocations. It is expected that mercenary elements may want to exploit the screening to create problems and the Party has therefore advised that we revolutionaries must fill the cinemas. First, to prevent such vile material from poisoning our people's minds and, second, to respond with revolutionary conviction to any provocation that may arise".

This is what happened: the film was shown, but except for the first three days when they were open to the general public, the rest of the screenings were viewed almost exclusively by members of the Communist Youth League, the Communist Party, the Association of Combatants of the Revolution and workers from state institutions who were mobilised to fill the cinemas (in many cases, as was learned later, those who attended that day received double pay). From that moment the cultural commissars launched a sustained smear campaign. At its head were Abel Prieto, president of UNEAC and future Minister of Culture, who repeated several times that 'Alice' was a poor quality film artistically, and Alfredo Guevara, who accused it of a political ambiguity unforgivable given the difficult situation of a country besieged by the United States and imperialism.

_ Against all bridges

The establishment of a vibrant Cuban cultural scene in exile, thanks to the contributions of thousands of artists of the Cuban diaspora that had begun in the early days of the Revolution, forced there to be a dialogue, a rapprochement, for one simple reason: after 30 years it was irrational and retrograde, when talking of Cuban culture, only to consider what was produced on the island. Something so obvious began to break down the many barriers that ideology and politics had erected between the ranks of Cuban artists, writers and intellectuals on what many of us called "las orillas de lo cubano" ("the two Cuban sides"). Thus emerged the need to rebuild bridges, open up channels of cross-fertilisation that would bind together again that single essence that political strategists, cultural commissars and gendarmes had split in two. It was not very difficult to achieve, because, as well as the spiritual bonds forged by our creativity springing from the same roots, those forming the tree of the nation, there were many connections (generational, friendships, literary trends and tendencies, experiential, stylistic, etc.), among those who engaged in the arts and thought in Cuba and those who did so in the diaspora.

That was just it: the severing of human connections (which are always stronger than ideological or political connections) had been a strategy of the Revolution, which adopted as a principle one of the traits of Fidel Castro's egocentric personality: the obsessive use of the maxim "Divide and rule". As has already been shown, in his long life Fidel managed to chalk up an astonishing tally of attacks on the unity and integrity of those who prevented him from achieving his goals. This warped behaviour was demonstrated even in his distant childhood with his own siblings, as is clear from the anecdotes told by his sister Juanita, his older brother Ramón, and even Raúl Castro himself.

Under that divisive rule, the Revolution would not allow any such cultural reunification to take place because it would lose him his absolute control of culture which, as has been mentioned, was one of his most powerful propaganda tools. Furthermore, some of the international sponsors of this attempt at reunification featured on the official blacklist of enemies of the "revolutionary process". It was therefore understandable that the Cuban government would have an interest in the failure of the events and projects which were all based on the naive belief that such dialogue could be possible with the involvement of the people who had thought of themselves as lords and masters of Cuban culture since 1959.

This explains why the meeting in Stockholm, in 1994, organised by the Olof Palme International Centre and coordinated by the Cuban exiled writer René Vázquez Díaz, only took place after lengthy and complex bureaucratic prodecures and, as several of the participants say to this day, it was a meeting thwarted in its central aim – to rebuild bridges. The same then happened with "La isla entera" ("The whole island"), a poetry symposium: participants from the island received their "exit permits" just 24 hours before their departure. Although the pressure on them from the political police and cultural commissars would strain their relations with their exiled colleagues at some points, in general there was a close and respectful relationship that irked the censors on the island. As a result, subsequent official analyses of the conference, in Cuba, would be poisoned by the belligerent and excluding language typical of the political leadership, who wished to prevent the experience being repeated.

They succeeded: the Berlin Cuban Literature Conference in 1995, after a long saga of complications lasting two months, was attended by only two writers from the island. The Festival of Nantes, also in 1995, which aimed to provide a complete overview of Cuban culture and to which had been invited hundreds of writers on the island and in exile, in the end could not be held because the Cuban government disagreed with the inclusion of some artists and writers which it considered direct enemies. "The short story in Cuban literature," a seminar organised in Madrid by the Ministry for International Cooperation and Latin America, in collaboration with the Casa de las Américas and the Faculty of Languages at the Complutense University, was held between 29 January and 2 February 1996. Although it was designed to be the continuation of the 1994 event on Cuban poetry, several of the most important invitees from the island could not attend, also because of the refusal of the Cuban censors.

As Ángel Santiesteban explained in the foreword, years later, in 2002, there were further attempts to foster a closer literary relationship between our colleagues on the island and in exile, in this case through the Plaza Major publishing house with its Cuban Culture Collection, conceived and directed by Patricia Gutiérrez Menoyo from Puerto Rico, for which I had the honour of being editor and general coordinator. However, we suffered so many pressures, bureaucratic traps, threats and coercion that finally, after four years of anguish and resistance, the project was forced to close.

_ A summary of bad news

This was also a stage when censorship and repression diversified but, most significantly, the official methods used to play down their impact on the cultural scene (and even more so, beyond it) became so expert and subtle that it was very difficult prove their existence. To reinforce this clever strategy, the Revolution's cultural spokesmen, headed by Abel Prieto (UNEAC president until 1997 when he was appointed Minister of Culture), began to use all the forums at their disposal to declare that anyone who talked about censorship and cultural

However, this wall of silence was broken down by some cases, interesting because of the reputation of those censored. The best-known were members of the Diaspora(s) literary group, an alternative writing project set up by Rolando Sánchez Mejías (1959) together with Carlos A. Aguilera (1970), Rogelio Saunders (1963), Pedro Marqués de Armas (1965), Ismael González

Castañer (1961), Ricardo Alberto Pérez (1963), José Manuel Prieto (1962) and Radamés Molina (1968), which became a reference point for Cuban literature between 1993 and 2002.

> According to Carlos A. Aguilera, Diaspora(s) had two stages, "one that starts in 1993 or 1994, when it aspires to be to be a mixture of terrorism and pedagogy" and "another that begins in 1997 with the publication of 'Diáspora(s). Documentos' ('Diaspora(s). Documents') magazine up to 2002. (...) The group has a dissident way of thinking and their discourses through poetry and essays have a lot of demolition power, as evidenced by the significant number of essays Rolando Sánchez Mejías, Rogelio Saunders, Pedro Marqués de Armas and Carlos A. Aguilera published in the journal. (...) With the essays, the authors draw attention to issues that had hitherto not been addressed in the official cultural media: fascism, violence, madness, totalitarianism, the difficult relationship with the national poetic tradition (...) The best-developed theme is resistance to nationalism, which cuts across all the genres used by these authors (...) Politically, they have set themselves apart from official institutions and have a tortured relationship with the Orígenes group... (...) Resistance to authoritarianism is central to the most avant-garde writing of Diaspora(s)".

The above extract, taken from the beginning of an article on the group by the critic Idalia Morejón Arnaiz in issue 148 of the Mexican magazine 'Crítica', makes it clear that, although Sanchez Mejias in his "Introduction" to the first issue of 'Diáspora(s). Documentos', stated that Diaspora(s) was "una avanzadilla (sin)táctica de guerra"[1], every one of its aims was a direct challenge to the Revolution's monopoly of power over life and its ossified concept of culture. As a result, starting with Sánchez Mejías, the group's intellectual leader, all of them could give a list here of the censorship and pressure

---

[1] Translator's note – una avanzadilla (sin)táctica de guerra – A deliberately ambiguous play on words – it could be interpreted as 'an advance party (without) war tactics' or as 'a syntactical advance party of war'.

they have suffered which have forced some of them to emigrate (Sánchez Mejías, Aguilera, Prieto, Molina), to marginalise themselves to avoid being cruelly marginalised by the regime (Pedro Marqués de Armas, Ricardo Alberto Pérez), or to become culture officials for the government like Ismael González Castañer.

In other cases, errors by censors and repressors who did not seem to be aware of the "new rules" to prevent scandals, allowed censorship, bans and strategies of repression to become known, at least in cultural circles.

The case of Guillermo Vidal Ortiz (1952-2004) was the most shameful, since it involved one of Cuba's best-loved and most respected writers because of his great humility despite being the author of one of the most original and authentic works of Cuban fiction. Guillermo was also devastatingly honest, deeply cultured and with a courage that he showed throughout his life. That honesty, which led him to question many of the injustices he experienced, began to filter into his work, doubly annoying the censors. They tried to buy his silence with trips and cultural posts: he refused to be bought. They tried to silence him by sending him literary teachers and friends he respected: he refused to keep quiet. Then they attacked him where it hurt most – his family – and wrongfully convicted Aliar, his youngest son, who was taken to prison and told that he would be released only if he convinced his father to silence his criticism. "I'm proud of your integrity and I remain proud of you, so don't worry about what they do to me in prison, just don't give in", was Aliar's response to Guillermo, and that bravery thwarted that repressive dirty tactic. I was Guillermo's best friend in his later years, to the point that he declared me his literary executor before he died of cancer.

The publisher has not allocated enough pages to me in this book for me to describe all the traps, pressure, and censorship he had to face, without it ever destroying that cheerfulness that all his friends still remember as one of his personal hallmarks. To mention just two of the most absurd plots against him, I could talk about a night at a literary event in Cienfuegos, where an alleged admirer, a beautiful girl of 16, was sent to him. She undressed in front of him and began to try and seduce him. As luck would have it, hours before, a friend had overheard a political police officer give the girl instructions to sleep with Guillermo. She was a minor, a camera had been put in the room and something like that would have destroyed Guillermo's reputation, as well as being the pretext they needed to put him behind bars. We were able to warn Guillermo and, when the girl was naked on the bed, he stood in front of where the camera would be and said, "The show's over. It's you who should be in prison for using a young girl for something so dirty. You should be ashamed yourselves for spending money to spy on people who just want to say what they think."

Or I could recall the huge crisis sparked in the Ministry of Culture by the decision of a worker in a printing press, retired from the Ministry of the Interior, who prevented his comrades from printing the novel 'El quinto sol' ('The Fifth Sun') by Guillermo Vidal, because he considered it counter-revolutionary. The book had just won the 1996 Hermanos Loynaz National Prize. In addition to threatening his comrades that they would be implicated in an act against Fidel Castro if they printed the novel, the old soldier sent a letter to the senior ranks of the armed forces, demanding that the writer be punished for his ideological deviancy and complaining that the Ministry of Culture awarded prizes to books attacking the Revolution. I witnessed the fear that permeated the senior management offices of the Cuban Book Institute and the Ministry of Culture and I can safely say that, rather than defend the writer, what they wanted was to escape unscathed from an unexpected attack. The writer Antón Arrufat, who we met at an event at the time, told several writers, including Guillermo, "What has happened has happened purely because this country has two ministries of culture: an official one without any real power, headed by our little comrade Abel Prieto and another in the shadows with the real power headed by men with a lot of stars on their shoulders."

Unfortunately, it would not be the only book to be withdrawn from the printers after being approved. Some examples, among some twenty known cases, are 'La noche del Gran Godo' ('The night of the great Goth') (UNEAC Short Story Prize, 1992), by Manuel Gayol Mecías, and 'Las largas horas de la noche' ('The long night hours') (finalist for the Casa de las Américas novel prize, 1993), by Antonio Álvarez Gil. The books' publication was halted because the authors had decided not to return to Cuba from their respective trips to Spain and Sweden. More than a hundred titles suffered from one of the dirtiest silencing strategies: the book was published in small editions, with the author deceived into believing it was a normal print run (in Cuba that was then 1000 to 3000 copies). A hundred or two hundred copies were distributed to the main bookshops visited by the author and a small number of copies went to the launch at the International Book Fair. That way, the author could not say he had been censored, but his book, with only 300 or 500 copies, would be totally invisible in a country of readers. While I was working at the Department of Literature at the Cuban Book Institute, I got to know of many "controversial" authors silenced with this ploy, but also "polemical" works by authors loyal to the government which received the same treatment. The cases I remember include Rafael Almanza, Antonio José Ponte, Eduardo del Llano, Jorge Ángel Pérez, Alejandro Aguilar, Pedro de Jesús, and Guillermo Vidal. Luckily, I was able to let several colleagues know in time that surplus copies of their books had been sent to a warehouse in Havana where they would be hidden until they were pulped, the most notorious case being 'Paisaje de Arcilla' ('Clay Landscape'), by Alejandro Aguilar, who was able to recover the copies in time thanks to my warning. (Unfortunately, my job became unbearable due to the pressure I began to feel and the distrust with which I was treated.)

Whenever I talk about these issues I am often asked how the government prevented foreign literature that did not meet their rigid standards reaching Cuban readers through international book fairs. What happened was that, for many years, the large international publishers also came to the island, even though financially (especially because of the price restrictions the state imposed on books) sales in Cuba were not significant. They stopped coming when some of those big publishers, attempting to exercise the right to promote exiled Cuban authors in their catalogue in the natural market for their books, began to apply for permits to sell on the island works by, for example, Zoé Valdés, Guillermo Cabrera Infante, Reinaldo Arenas, Daína Chaviano. Aware of Cuban readers' desire to access literature banned for reasons they thought absurd, in these applications the publishers included works such as '1984' and 'Animal Farm' by George Orwell and 'The Gulag Archipelago' by Alexander Solzhenitsyn. These applications, put simply, were the excuse the censors needed to ban these publishers from Cuban book fairs. "We can not allow them to inject us with subversion through literature", Omar González, then president of the Cuban Book Institute, told a meeting in 1997.

In those years, control of foreign literature, or Cuban literature published outside the island, ran (and still runs today) through a complex mechanism: the exchange of information by the institutions linked to the International Book Fair (Ministry of Culture, *Casa de las Américas, Ediciones Cubanas* (Cuban Publishing), *Cámara Cubana del Libro* (Cuban Book Chamber), *Agencia Literaria Latinoamericana* (Latin American Literary Agency) and *Oficina de Publicaciones Periódicas* (Office of Periodicals)), advised by state security experts and with the collaboration of the customs department. The collaboration that enabled books banned or worthy of censorship to be identifed and sifted out started from the first exchange between the Cuban Book Chamber and the publishers applying to attend the Fair. An essential step was the requirement for a comprehensive customs statement of what they wanted to bring into the country, which included, obviously, a list of titles. All this information, once gathered and organised, was processed by various working groups and, once decisions had been made on the material to be allowed in or rejected, strategies would be drawn up, varying according to the complexity and importance of the publishing houses concerned. In many cases, when there were doubts about certain works and certain authors, a committee of readers from the Cuban Book Institute would have to quickly read the titles subject to doubts and determine whether or not to allow their presence at the fair. Generally, except on very few occasions, the censored publishers never found out. Strategies to prevent the entry of prohibited material could range from delaying their customs clearance, unexpected and exaggerated rises in prices for hiring services or stands for publishers who were bringing in "controversial" works, to bureaucratic measures that the organisers had ostensibly had to take "at the last minute". It is a curious fact (but after reading all that happened in this period many will feel that it was logical) that it was in these years that there was the biggest exodus of artists and writers since the stampedes of the 1960s and the departures via Mariel port in 1980. Just to use an example close to my heart, over 70% of the last two generations of writers and artists (those who developed in the 1980s and early 1990s), would leave the island between 1991 and 2003: by taking advantage of invitations to events outside the island; by setting off by sea (unfortunately, many did not succeed and were drowned or eaten by sharks, like one of my best students, the young writer Laylí Pérez Negrín); by having the luck to win the US visa lottery, or as part of the rafter migration crisis in 1994, when over 36,000 Cubans left the country in makeshift boats. They fortified the already strong Cuban cultural presence in the United States (mainly Miami) and Spain (especially Madrid and Barcelona), cities that, without any doubt, have become the capitals of Cuban culture in the diaspora.

The Roman arena of the mercenaries

It is sad but true: writers, artists and intellectuals from the island passively (and in some cases complicitly) accepted all the acts of censorship and repression in this period for various reasons, ranging from lack of information, opportunism, feuds between group (if repression was against a member of another literary or artistic clique there was no reason to meddle) to fear.

As has been said, it was a period when independent journalism was the most active expression of popular discontent. Across the country, individual voices of Cubans began to be heard. Though most had not received formal training, they became journalists, trying with their articles to reflect the reality concealed by the official press. Then, through a confluence of interests, opposition working groups and projects began to emerge, such as the CubaPress agency, founded by the poet and journalist Raúl Rivero Castañeda (one of the signatories of the Letter of the Ten) and Ricardo González Alfonso, who founded in 2001 the *Sociedad de Periodistas Manuel Márquez Sterling* (Manuel Márquez Sterling Journalists Association) and 'De Cuba' magazine in 2002. The news agency Decoro Working Group also had a prominent role. One of its founders, the writer, journalist and editor

Armando Añel describes it thus:

> "... It emerged in the summer of 1998. It was founded by
> journalists including Manuel Vázquez Portal (president), Claudia
> Márquez Linares, Armando Añel and Héctor Maseda. The group
> produced reports primarily for CubaNet news agency, based in
> Miami, and Radio Martí, as well as others. At the beginning, the
> group had about ten members, most of them young. I think this
> feature, youth, as well as a certain literary flavour to much of their
> work (articles and essays), gave the group a distinctive identity
> in the world of the independent Cuban press. In 1999 the Cuban
> regime drew up Law 88, the "Gagging Law", and when it was
> passed some of these young people left the group, fearing a raid
> and subsequent imprisonment."

These, and other groups of opposition journalists, have the merit of having
formed a large bloc of journalists who managed to get their work out of
the island and raise international awareness of the Cuban people's trauma.
However, generally, their work was little known and their reports had little
mobilising effect on the island itself.

That work within Cuban society would be spearheaded by what I regard
as the greatest project for social thought and civic work in society that has
ever existed: 'Vitral' ('Stained-glass window'), a magazine and cultural project
in Pinar del Río, run by a lay intellectual, Dagoberto Valdés. From 1994, when
the magazine's first issue was published with the support of Monsignor
José Ciro Bacallao, bishop of Pinar del Río, until its shameful closure in
2007 as one of the Catholic Church's concessions to Raúl's government,
seeking to secure more space for the development of Catholicism in Cuba,
the magazine's 120 issues published a series of highly significant essays and
analyses of national problems from a deeply critical perspective. The project
also gave exposure to censored writers and intellectuals through the pages of
this magazine, through the Vitral publishing house, and literary prizes with
the same name. For four years I had the privilege of working with Dagoberto
Valdés and his team as a member of the jury for the prize. As well as the

harassment and marginalisation suffered by the great painter Pedro Pablo Oliva for defending the Vitral project, I witnessed many other pressures, threats and acts of coercion by the political police, powerless against the increasing influence that this civic project's purity, ethics and honesty were gaining within the province, the intelligentsia and the country. I could provide a list here of the writers who, because of Vitral's prestige, agreed to serve as jury members but who, at the last minute, apologised to me because they lacked the courage to defy the menacing warnings from political police officers who had "suggested" that they did not work with that "mercenary rats' nest" (words that "kindly" convinced a well-known dramatist not to be on the jury).

However, the biggest scandal in this period would be the Black Spring of 2003, to which I shall refer very briefly as it has already received a lot of international coverage because of its importance as one of the lowest points in terms of violations against freedom of expression in Cuba. Nevertheless, I will add, as an interesting detail, which I found out after the trials of some fellow journalists with whom I had clandestine conversations in those days, that it all erupted when the political police sent Fidel Castro a video in which some independent journalists working with US newspapers commented to an American official at the US Interests Section office that support for dissidents should be increased because journalism had now become so powerful that not even Fidel Castro himself could stop it. That was their mistake: not knowing that you can not claim that Fidel is defeated because he takes it as a personal challenge.

From 18 to 20 March 2003, taking advantage of US President George Bush's approval of the military attack on Iraq to defeat Saddam Hussein, just over a hundred dissidents were arrested, 75 of whom would be sentenced to long prison terms, and for some of them (Martha Beatriz Roque Cabello and José Daniel Ferrer) the revolutionary prosecutors even demanded the death penalty.

Such disproportionate repression came, however, to have a global impact that the Cuban government did not expect, with strong criticism even from many of the most nostalgic international supporters of Fidel

Castro's dictatorship. The mostly summary trials lacked any of the necessary procedural guarantees. It was obvious that the accused had been convicted in advance, although the (later dethroned) Foreign Minister, Felipe Pérez Roque, told the foreign press that everything had been conducted with the utmost legality and that the rights of each of the defendants had been respected to the letter (later it was discovered that most had only met their lawyer shortly before the trial and did not even know the sentences requested by the prosecution).

As we know, a few years later, due to international pressure and discussions held by the Catholic Church and Spain with the Cuban government, after suffering imprisonment in such dreadful conditions that many of them became seriously ill (Miguel Valdés Tamayo, Oscar Manuel Espinosa Chepe and Antonio Augusto Villareal Acosta would die as a result of these illnesses), these prisoners would be sent into forced exile (they were told that they would be released only if they agreed to leave the country), except for 12 who refused to emigrate and still remain in Cuba.

The most serious damage inflicted by the Black Spring was in removing the leaders of a national information platform that becoming dangerous to the dictatorship. Although this would sow the seeds for an awakening of civic consciousness and of important sectors of independent civil society (especially with the public actions of the movement now known as the "Damas de Blanco" ("Ladies in White")), the atmosphere became even tenser, darkening the country with a climate of fear. This was particularly acute in the spheres of culture and journalism when Fidel Castro announced that he would come down with an iron fist on those who had been freely defaming the Revolution and announced that his magnanimity had come to an end. In the latent threats of his words, he made it clear that those convicted that spring would not be the only ones.

CHAPTER III
THE DYING BITES...

The last three years of the Fidel Era (2003-2006) and the ten years of the Raulist Era are so called because they are two clearly distinguishable historical periods in terms of their strategies for politics, economics and international relations, but can be treated as a single period as far as culture is concerned because the strategy for censorship and repression has been so static.

Since the events of the Black Spring in 2003, Cuban culture has undergone a strange metamorphosis. While it is true that, at the end of the 1980s and in the 1990s, with some exceptions, the censors' and repressors' subtle behaviour made many people believe that there was openness and official permissiveness in art and culture, it is also undeniable that, in the course of these past thirteen years, the official cultural institutions lost credibility, and began to be seen as appendages of the regime, completely hamstrung by politics and ideology. The entrenchment of these institutions by the side of the political leadership at critical moments for the artists and writers whom they were supposed to defend eventually destroyed the false image of representativeness that they had enjoyed one point, and they were becoming simple travel agencies (UNEAC, Hermanos Saíz Association, Ministry of Culture), forbidden territory difficult to access (national publishers and the International Book Fair, in the case of literature) or unimportant spaces, providing consolation, (small and backward provincial publishers and regional book fairs) given that other arenas were impossible to access, reserved for has-beens and "faithful sheep".

Two major developments have emerged. On the one hand, there has been an explosion in an alternative form of creativity where the artist produces work divorced from any institutions or the body of artists (the independent blogosphere, for example), and on the other hand, the cultural commissars and institutions' focus, in their rhetoric, on defending the "national essence" from "neocolonial" attacks by an alleged fifth column financed by the enemies of the Cuban Revolution. The clearest evidence has been the increasing politicisation of the Havana International Book Fair over the years, making the event one of the biggest promoters of ALBA, the ideological project devised by Venezuela's ex-president Hugo Chávez and Fidel Castro in 2004. However, it must also be added that the ALBA Cultural project, based in Havana with branches in the member countries of this group, has served to attract artists by offering them opportunities for publication and promotion (subtly conditional on political support for the project) in the case of Latin America; and to silence the discontent of Cuban artists on the island (with travel and periods of "cultural cooperation" in ALBA countries), and also to recruit significant sections of the international intelligentsia.

The censorship discourse has focused on promoting the idea that there are designs to destroy the revolution and the socialist project in Latin America through a coordinated international plan to confuse important figures in literature, art and thought on the island, making them act as a fifth column. It is significant that those words begin to appear frequently from 2004 in speeches and interviews given to the national and international press by all five political commissars linked to the promotion of cultural policy from then to the present day: the writer Abel Prieto (Pontiff of censorship and repression in Cuba for the last three decades), the engineer and journalist Iroel Sánchez (ex-president of the Cuban Book Institute, who works in the Oficina para la Informatización de la Sociedad Cubana (Office for the Computerisation of Cuban Society), writer and philosopher Eliades Acosta Matos (who served as Head of the Department of Culture for the Party's Central Committee until he was sacked), Fernando Rojas (current Deputy Minister of Culture) and writer Miguel Barnet, UNEAC's current president.

It should be made clear that it was logical that this label, "fifth columnists", should be adopted. To this day, the Cuban government brands as "mercenaries" all those enemies with direct links to US agencies or officials in Havana or outside the island, and that label usually has more of a political basis. However, in Cuba, in the early years of this century, policymakers did not know how to classify, nor what form of attack to adopt with the many writers, artists and intellectuals who had managed to do our work independently of state-sponsored institutions (in my case, through European publishers thanks to my literary agent Ray Güde Mertin). Despite our criticisms, they could not pigeonhole us as "mercenaries" because most of us had strongly rebuffed the approaches of officials from the US Interests Section in Havana. It is generally thought that the refusal of the island's cultural world to have anything to do with that US mission is due to fear of repression. Although it can not be denied that many have that fear, in many other cases (such as mine), I rejected them despite having received many invitations, because, apparently proud of their stupidity, misunderstanding and ignorance of the cultural sector, those representatives "of the empire" treated us like lackeys when they approached us, showing no respect for our ideas and imposing in advance the conditions for the "help" they could offer. For that reason, the censors needed to cling onto the term "fifth columnists" so they could pigeonhole us somehow in their framework of control. Their idea was that we were confused, misinformed, and that prevented us from seeing that our demands and criticism of the government played into the hands of the enemies of what should be "our social project".

There were, and still are, times when many cases of censorship and repression do not receive the condemnation from cultural circles that they should. This can be attributed to the misinformation within the island, the policy of sowing fear (now not just of tacit repression but also and especially of the doors being closed on professional fulfilment: "In Cuba you know you have to keep your head down if you want to get published and they make you believe that outside the island you'll die as a writer from the greed of capitalism", says the writer Rafael Vilches Proenza in a recent letter). There is also the political exploitation of the divisions between artists through the silent encouragement of wars between groups and cliques ("We all know that giving support to Heras' school [writer Eduardo Heras León, founder of the Onelio Jorge Cardoso National Literary Training Centre] is a strategy to weaken the group called the *Lobby Gay* (Gay Lobby) which is very critical of cultural policy," continues Vilches), and the old policy of discrediting artists who challenge or criticise the government through fabrications or half truths. However, it is also the case that the docility that most writers, artists and intellectuals have shown for decades in the face of the outrages of repression and censorship has so reduced the limited role that they could play as intermediaries between society and the government that they have not been heard even in those few cases when they have tried to defend their colleagues.

I will take advantage of the fact that information on many of the instances of censorship and cultural repression on the island, in this period, is easily available on the internet, and will try to briefly focus on the cases that have had national repercussions, and also international, the latter especially in recent years thanks to new technologies.

_ Summary of more bad news

As Ángel Santiesteban explains in the foreword, the official reaction to one of my books and to one of the cultural projects in which I had a prominent role are considered two of the dictatorship's most despicable acts of repression in the early twenty-first century. They are known as the Havana Babylon Affair (the repercussions of which lasted from 1999 until my exile in 2005) and the Affair of the Cuban Culture Collection of Patricia Gutiérrez Menoyo (2002-2005). However, these were not the only bruises left by the strong arm of censorship and repression of Fidel Castro's government (first) and Raul (from 2006 to present).

As I mentioned in the previous chapter, the integrity of Monsignor José Siro González Bacallao, bishop of Pinar del Río and the dedication of the lay intellectual Dagoberto Valdés made it possible for an annoying thorn of free opinion and independence to stick in the regime's side for several years: the Vitral civic project. The death blow came with the talks between the Vatican and Havana: first, the bishop's retirement was announced, then the retirement of Archbishop Pedro Meurice, Archbishop of Santiago de Cuba ("coincidentally", the only two openly critical of the Castro dynasty and its abuses of power). Then came the replacement of these two prelates by docile bishops, which removed any obstacles to the closure of *Vitral* magazine, publishing house and civic project in 2007, by decree of the Cuban Catholic Church led by Cardinal Jaime Ortega. Neither Dagoberto Valdés nor any of the other leaders of this project gave up and they founded the magazine '*Convivencia*' ('Coexistence'), another space for the free exchange of ideas, which is harassed, repressed and censored to this day.

Determined to defend its monopoly on information, the Cuban political police focused on controlling or destroying the many independent magazines that emerged in those years. In some cases, they distorted or maintained a tight rein on what was published by infiltrating undercover agents into these magazines, some of whom who even became senior managers (basically this applied to publications, newspapers and news agencies of the political opposition). In other cases, those accused of being "fifth columnists" would be young writers who had established literary or cultural magazines without the permission of the institutions that the Ministry of Culture had for this purpose. In these cases, the censorship strategy deployed other methods: a "conversation" with the management to convince them that their naivety had made them serve as a fifth column; brief prison terms with beatings to frighten them (as happened with the writer Jorge Luis Arzola, in Ciego de Ávila) or harsh sentences (writer Reinaldo Hernández Soto spent 7 years behind bars from 1995); house searches to confiscate banned literature or equipment; physical threats and possible criminal prosecution for breaching Law 88 (the Gagging Law). These procedures were used to censor, among others, '*Cacharro(s)*' by the fiction writer Jorge Alberto Aguiar in Havana, '*Bifronte*' magazine and the writers who coalesced around it under the leadership of the poet, novelist and freelance journalist Luis Felipe Rojas Rosabal in Holguín, and any of the work (publications, videos, performances, etc.) of the *Omni-Zona Franca* project, led by Luis Eligio Pérez, Amaury Pacheco, David Escalona, Alina Guzmán, Nilo Julián González and Juan Carlos Flores.

Particularly in the period from 2000 until 2009, when internal divisions split the project '*Encuentro de la Cultura Cubana*' ('Encounter of Cuban Culture') into two (forming 'Cubaencuentro' and 'Diario de Cuba'), this atmosphere of fear and threats spread to other writers in Cuba who expressed a desire to write for magazines run by Cuban exiles and to be paid for this work. At a meeting, commissar Eliades Acosta Matos would call it "a weakness for the enemy's currency". Accusations of being cultural fifth columnists were therefore levelled at many of us who worked on the magazine and project 'Encuentro de la Cultura Cubana' (the publication that the dictatorship considered intellectual enemy number one, founded by writer Jesús Díaz and directed by him until his death in 2002); its successor, the 'Cubaencuentro' website; 'Revista Hispano-Cubana' ('Hispano-Cuban Journal') in Madrid and the 'Diario de Cuba' ('Cuba Daily') website.

In addition to these less traumatic strategies of applying pressure to prevent collaboration with "publications funded by the enemy" (the justification most used by the political commissars), strategies that in some cases resulted in writers who wrote for these magazines in defiance of the censors being sacked or refused employment in cultural institutions, the most outrageous act of repression was targeted at the poet, novelist and essayist Antonio José Ponte. As well as his clearly anti-government stance and statements, Ponte had had the audacity, living in Cuba, to agree to being a member of the editorial board of 'Encuentro' ('Encounter') magazine. A writer admired for the quality of his work, and an intellectual respected for the ethics and independence with which he always defended his ideas, Ponte became the favourite target of attacks not only by the cultural commissars, but also by those middle- and low-level officials in cultural institutions who regarded him as an arch-enemy.

Although there is a lot of information on the internet about the repression he suffered while living in Cuba (repression that would eventually force him into exile), I must point out that we were all moved by his courage in confronting the two main commissars at that time – Abel Prieto (then Minister of Culture) and Iroel Sánchez (president of the Cuban Book Institute) at a meeting of writers; I must add that this courage provoked a backlash by the cultural officials who proposed his "deactivation" as a member of UNEAC (a term which sought to soften the word "expulsion"); and also add that this was the first time that the UNEAC's management had imposed such an egregious form of censorship. They completely ignored the official complaints made against this punishmen by a group of writers and intellectuals, including the poet Reina María Rodríguez (since awarded the National Prize for Literature for her life and work), whose arguments were notable for their clarity and cogency. For these same sins, and for their critical reflections on Cuban reality, some writers would be totally excluded from the official cultural system: the most representative cases to date are the poets Rafael Alcides and Rafael Almanza, two essential names in Cuban literature.

Neither was cinema immune from notorious cases of censorship in this period. In 2004, the daring of writer and director Eduardo del Llano would focus the attention of the censors, this time for his short film *Monte Rouge*, which openly ridiculed the Cuban police. Two officers knock on an artist's door and announce that they have come to instal microphones so they can hear his anti-government conversations with his fellow artists. From that moment on an atmosphere of absurdity is created which mocks police control, state corruption and the fear that the government has instilled in every Cuban for decades. This self-funded film features cinema and television actors well-known on the island and that made it even more daring, so no-one was surprised at the pressure that was then exerted. Unfortunately, in statements he made to try and prevent his case "being manipulated" abroad or by enemies of the Revolution, Eduardo del Llano killed off the significance that his work could have gained in the fight against censorship. It was he himself, with his conciliatory words (which many believe were full of fear), who muffled the critical impact that *Monte Rouge*'s clandestine distribution was having on those people who were seeking a way of escaping the prevailing atmosphere of prohibition in the artistic and cultural world at that time.

Had the door which Del Llano opened with his short fim and closed with his remarks remained open, it would have paved the way for "cinema's adaptation to changes in critical thinking and to the questioning climate of the new times that can already be seen in other art forms", which Fernando Pérez referred to in a discussion during the Havana International Film Festival in 2005, when analysing the history of the struggle by Cuban artists and producers to achieve greater freedom in filmmaking. According to many articles on these events, it is possible that steps would have been taken (as some filmmakers tried to do, taking advantage of Monte Rouge's critical success) that would have prevented the ban on the national distribution of 'La vaca de mármol' ('The marble cow'), a documentary by Enrique Colina, made in 2013, an irreverent look at the government's propaganda concerning Ubre Blanca (White Udder), a cow that was said to have produced a hundred litres of milk a day; or censorship of 'Crematorio' 'Crematorium', a film by Juan Carlos Cremata, produced independently in the same year, 2013. At some points in these articles or interviews (I recall articles by Juan Antonio García, Enrique Colina, Cremata, and interviews by the actor Jorge Perugorría, directors Fernando Pérez and Ernesto Daranas and the writer Leonardo Padura) it is suggested that the reason censorship still dominates the cinema and audiovisual worlds is because of disunity, the lack of agreed lines of criticism supported in sufficient numbers, and the artists' failure to unite when they should have done to oppose the censorship of a particular work. That would explain the censors' "misunderstandings" that led to temporary censorship and debates over 'Return to Ithaca', a film by French director Laurent Cantet, scripted by Leonardo Padura, winner of the Princess of Asturias Award for Literature, and the cloak of silence thrown over the international success of the film 'El rey de La Habana' 'The king of Havana', based on a book by another internationally-famous Cuban writer whose work has been censored in Cuba, Pedro Juan Gutiérrez, both scandals which occurred as recently as 2015.

Although abroad there is the impression that the "changes" made by Raúl Castro have definitively opened the doors to freedom of expression ("Cubans now openly criticise the government", "people are no longer afraid", "nobody is punished for saying what they think even if it is against the government", according to many newspapers around the world), it is important to stress that, although repression is now not always targeted at the isolated individual who is publicly critical, there is still repression and persecution of anyone whose criticism may lead to public protests or who organises and forms groups to provide a more effective channel for denouncing the regime. Under this strategy (which stands out because the attacks come together under a single label – "fifth column mercenaries") there has been constant repression of three opposition projects that have sought to have an impact on society with proposals including raising political consciousness and the strengthening of a civil society not controlled by the dictatorship:

> 'Primavera Digital' ('Digital Spring') the first opposition newspaper addressing the world from Cuba. It is managed by journalists Juan González Febles and Luis Cino, based on an idea in 2005. It went live on 22 November 2007 and from 2012 began to print and distribute copies on the island. They have also been pioneers in exposing the situation in Cuba through blogs it has hosted since its inception, the most notable being 'Círculo Cínico' by Luis Cino and 'Infierno de Palo' by Juan González Febles.

14yMedio, a digital publication founded in Havana on 21 May 2014, by Cuban blogger Yoani Sánchez and her husband, journalist Reinaldo Escobar. Although it has failed to reach a wide readership on the island, this website has been gaining exposure through its journalism, while having to fight not only against the regime's tactics of destruction, computer blocking and defamation, but also against the doubts about the project provoked by the blogger's controversial personality and the conflicting opinions about her across the Cuban political spectrum, both on the island and in exile. Some see her as a heroine of the Cuban opposition; others, supporting the dictatorship, consider her, her blog, 'Generación Y' ('Generation Y') and 14ymedio as a monstrosity financed from abroad; and others (enemies of Castroism) think it is a Trojan horse within the opposition, infiltrated by Castro's political police to upstage other opposition projects internationally, while confusing the world by projecting an image of tolerance. "Even a mercenary like Yoani Sánchez enjoys the right that the revolution has given her to found her own newspaper", Bruno Rodríguez Parrilla, the Cuban Foreign Minister, said in a recent interview. All this controversy has made it difficult for 14yMedio to increase its readership, already limited by the simple fact that, out of a population of 11.2 million, only 2 million have internet access, and in most cases this access is expensive, limited and sporadic.

Estado de Sats (State of Sats), a project founded in July 2010 by the activists Antonio Rodiles and Ailer González, to create a forum for participation and debate for Cuban civil society. Its most important contribution from a cultural point of view has been to give a public voice (in videos and open discussions) to marginalised or silenced Cuban opposition intellectuals, with the aim of providing an opportunity for debating the official intellectual discourse. Unfortunately, so far, instead of a debate, its activities and audiovisual materials have been forums for opponents from different tendencies to present their usually similar views on topical issues relating to the national reality; the project has failed to include, for example, divergent voices (from the blogosphere, political intelligentsia or the government itself) who believe that the Cuban social model must be reformed from within. However, Estado de Sats is currently the most heavily repressed, for its role in uniting opposition groups through projects such as the Foro por los Derechos y las Libertades (Forum for Rights and Freedoms), the #TodosMarchamos (WeAllMarch) campaign and the national and international publicity it gives every Sunday to the marches of the Ladies in White in Havana.

However, it is important to stress that censorship and repression is not restricted to publications and opposition groups whose projects involve culture or the promotion of thought. In view of the dictatorship's increasing inability to impose censorship without causing scandals or tarnishing the tolerant image it has devised to deceive the world, it has adopted the tactic of criminalising and defaming writers, accusing them of being fifth column collaborators, particularly when their criticisms achieve publicity outside the island, either through their own blogs or through "enemy" cultural projects abroad.

That has been the case for writers Ángel Santiesteban Prats and Rafael Vilches Proenza, visual artists Danilo Maldonado and Tania Bruguera, and director Juan Carlos Cremata, to give only some very recent examples. Ángel Santiesteban, the most distinguished Cuban short story writer of my generation, was sentenced to 5 years' imprisonment, falsely accused of domestic violence. Rafael Vilches, also a writer, was turned into an unemployed pariah through an intensive national campaign denigrating him for "wanting to find cultural validation by linking himself to mercenary projects and well-known dissident figures". Danilo Maldonado, a young visual artist, was imprisoned because of an absurd, personality cult-inspired regulation, under which historical leaders of the revolution are untouchable even for art. Tania Bruguera, best-known outside the island as a performance artist, was prevented from returning to the United States (where she lives), in reality accused of colluding in a plot to destabilise the dialogue accords between Cuba and the United States, although officially she was accused of "resisting authority and public disorder". Filmmaker and theatre director Juan Carlos Cremata suffered the censorship of a play he had staged and was sacked along with the other members of the theatre company. He is still attacked for "publicising internationally what happened to him, seeking the international attention which he has failed to gain with his work", say the cultural commissars.

The two most outrageous cases, because of the severity of the repression, were Danilo Maldonado and Ángel Santiesteban. The first of these was imprisoned for "public disorder" for trying to conduct performance art in the streets of Havana, walking two pigs painted green with "Fidel" and "Raúl" written in red letters on their backs. Despite never being tried, he was kept in prison for 10 months. He was released following an international campaign after he decided to go on hunger strike until he died or was set free.

With the second, Santisteban, the repression was even fiercer, "to make him pay for his treachery" as one of his jailers would say, because until 2007 he had been one of the writers most promoted by the regime, despite the fact that his works always had to undergo the tortures of censorship before they could see the light of day. However, Santiesteban, tired of pretending and keeping silent about his views on the destruction of the island, started a blog with the help of friends abroad. In his posts he began to show the hard life of Cubans and expose a host of shameful truths that the government was trying to conceal from the world. Fellow writers were sent to tell him to stop writing those posts; political police officers harassed him week after week, trying to convince him to abandon his dissident stance; they sent other (plainclothes) officers to give him a beating which broke his arm and one of them said to him, "That's what you get for being a counter-revolutionary"; the cultural authorities imposed a total ban on his work and on his participation in any kind of official events; he was prevented from attending an international event to which he had been invited in Puerto Rico, accused of crimes that were then proved false; the official TV programme 'Razones de Cuba' accused him of being an enemy of the Revolution... and all this only made his posts even more critical. Finally, they managed to convince his former wife and mother of one of his children to accuse him of having raped, beaten, robbed and tried to burn her alive. He was criminalised to such an extent that the prosecution asked for him to be sentenced to over 50 years' imprisonment. However, all the evidence was fake and Santiesteban was able to take apart the huge lie constructed to try and convict him. Finally, given the total lack of evidence, a handwriting expert working for the political police, after analysing a piece of Santiesteban's writing, concluded that he "could be" guilty because the slant of his letters demonstrated that he "could be" violent. With this "proof" he was sentenced to 5 years, of which he served half. Even in prison, he found ways to write and send critical posts for his blog. He is currently on probation, demanding a review of the judgment. This would clear him because his son, now an adult, confessed on foreign television that his mother had forced him to lie about his father, and psychologists from the political police had also pressured him to do so. Although he is no longer behind bars, Ángel Santiesteban remains a proscribed person on the island.

Finally, I could not end this brief summary without mentioning two events that shook the cultural scene from 2005, the emergence of the Cuban blogosphere, and in 2007, the greatest intellectual protest ever, known as "*La guerrita de los Emails*" ("The little war of emails") or "Pavongate ".

_ 2005 – The Cuban blogosphere

Like anything to do with internet technology, blogging came late to Cuba, but it only needed a few independent journalists to discover its potential as a tool for free expression for it to spread throughout the island. Yoani Sánchez's blog, 'Generation Y', is now well known because of its international impact and the controversy it has created. It is fair to say that it is partly due to her work that what was first called the "Blogger Movement" (referring to opposition blogs) emerged. The preferred name is the "Cuban blogosphere", seeking to encapsulate a phenomenon that may have been (and still is in many ways) Cuba's only arena for public debate on issues of national interest. In this virtual environment the ideas of those who oppose the dictatorship and those who defend it come together.

Although blogging is now a fairly wide and diverse phenomenon, it is important to stress the leading role played by the blogs of Yoani Sánchez, Claudia Cadelo, Orlando Luis Pardo Lazo, Ángel Santiesteban, Luis Felipe Rojas Rosabal and Luis Cino, among many others. These blogs, despite the serious difficulties in accessing the internet, sprung up throughout the island. Between 2005 and 2010, it was the '*Desde Cuba*' ('From Cuba') site (desdecuba.com) which gave the highest international profile to the bloggers using that platform, and the contributions of the magazines '*Voces*', '*Vitral*' and '*Primavera Digital*' also made a significant impact. As noted by writer and journalist Armando Añel in his article "Citizen journalism inside and outside Cuba" on the '*Blogger Cubano*' website, the most remarkable feature of this form of communication is that it "took the baton from traditional independent journalism (...) In the emerging era of social networking, the citizen journalism of the new bloggers was better adapted to the technological revolution under way. In parallel, a dynamic and varied movement of exiled bloggers served as a support to the bloggers in Cuba, and acted as a channel for the exchange of information during those years".

As Añel rightly states, the campaign on 1 June 2009, organised by Cuban bloggers in exile, was an important development, and one which I believe was the last straw for the censors. It had an impact on thousands of internet users from other countries, showing them the true repressive face of the dictatorship which was presented with three fundamental demands: the release of political prisoners, the lifting of restrictions on Cubans leaving and entering their country, and free access to the internet on the island.

The government decided to combat what official propaganda began to label a "media war" or, as journalist Randy Alonso called it in a television debate "fifth column journalism". In an attempt to respond to this supposed war, measures were adopted in three areas. First, the (controlled) emergence of pro-government bloggers was authorised as a counterweight to the opposition bloggers. Second, Cuban journalists began to be trained in the new technologies (many of them had not even been on the internet before) and they were required to provide pro-government responses whenever they found opinions in "enemy" blogs that should be addressed. Third, a division was formed at the University of Computer Sciences to counter attacks from the internet, not only from the enemy blogosphere, but also from any publication or website criticising the Revolution.

Some videos were leaked from an event on this subject organised by the Cuban political police, where experts explained the need to use all kinds of techniques (there was talk, for example, of robots, fake accounts, interception of e-mails, and hacking into accounts) in order to counter the international exposure the internet provided for counter-revolutionary ideas through, in the exact words of one of those experts, "fifth column tactics which in recent years have been frequently used by the US government in its attacks against us". At one of those conferences, an idea was suggested which we would then see explode onto the internet: not only revolutionaries living on the island had to become "cyber warriors", but also Cuban embassies had to recruit Cubans in exile to be turned into cyber warriors. The embassies were also expected to pressure foreign groups supporting the Revolution into getting their members to respond forcefully to any counter-revolutionary attack on the internet. In line with this tactic, Cuban diplomatic missions began to distribute numerous materials for a concerted smear campaign targeting all the opposition activists, groups and politicians who most frequently appeared on or used social media to show the civilised world the true face of the regime. It is these arguments that the cyber warriors normally deploy in social media to defend the Cuban Revolution. That period of confrontation through crude smear tactics resulted in a Kafkaesque situation: even the most prominent pro-government bloggers and journalists criticised the ideological entrenchment, lack of creativity and rigid concepts of freedom that limited them. They felt shackled by the rules they had to observe when defending the revolution if they were not to be censored themselves. Subsequently, coinciding with the thaw in relations between Havana and Washington, the waters of the blogosphere became calmer until 2015. That was when a group of those bloggers, critical of the regime but defenders of Cuban socialism, after being invited to find out about journalism in Germany, would be attacked by their own colleagues on the island, who accused them of being naive ("*ingenuos*", a label used in several posts) and incapable of seeing that they were being used in the strategy to destroy the Revolution through fifth column methods using information.

_ 2007 – The little war of emails
Recently, after the censorship of the play *Exit the King*, staged by El Ingenio theatre group, directed by Juan Carlos Cremata; after this talented artist was dismissed from his post and the actors "relocated" to other theatre companies, a group of filmmakers organised a public act of collective independence which, although it should be normal, is a rare beast in the

Cuban cultural world. First, the participants openly opposed the cultural commissars' crackdown on Cremata and questioned their claim that the artist had resigned himself to the censorship; then they deeply criticised the repressive control stifling creative freedoms and chaining directors and actors to the monopoly conceived by ICAIC, and to leave no doubt about their determination, they objected when an official tried to expel from the event Eliécer Ávila, a well-known leader of the political opposition movement Somos+, who was in the audience. However, it remains to be seen whether the criticisms made at this event resulted in repression or in solutions to the serious problems discussed there.

Something similar, but wider repercussions, occurred in January 2007. Unexpectedly, tributes were being paid on popular Cuban television programmes to former cultural commissars directly responsible for the repression of the "five grey years" of the 1970s. In late 2006, the Cuban Institute of Radio and Television (ICRT), then headed by Lieutenant Colonel Ernesto López (former director of Film Studies at the Ministry of the Armed Forces), had included in the television schedules an interview with Jorge "Papito" Serguera who, as has been been mentioned, was a prominent censor and the head of Cuban television between 1967 and 1974 at the height of the intellectual repression. On another programme there was an interview with Armando Quesada, known in the cultural world as "Torquesada",[2] as he had been the commissar in charge of the "revolutionary" task of purging Cuban theatre, in the course of which he closed the prestigious Puppet Theater and even ordered the dolls and puppets to be burnt.

Although these appearances rang alarm bells, especially among artists who had suffered repression at the hands of Serguera or Quesada, there was no reaction apart from an occasional exchange of comments between the victims. However, on 5 January 2007, Cubavisión, Cuban television's main channel, presented another repressor, the writer Luis Pavón Tamayo, on Impronta, a programme which, from its inception, had been designed to honour figures who deserved to be remembered forever in the history of Cuban culture. Luis Pavón Tamayo had chaired the sinister National

---

2 Translator's note – "Torquesada" – a play on words – a reference to Torquemada, Spain's first Grand Inquisitor

Council of Culture (CNC) between 1971 and 1976, and was considered one of the masterminds and executive arms of the repression, censorship and marginalisation of hundreds of artists, writers, intellectuals and journalists Cubans who would die without being vindicated, flee into exile or spend long years as social outcasts.

No one believed the line then put about that the tributes were due to "errors by misinformed specialists". To this day, no one can say what the people behind this manoeuvre were trying to achieve by raising dark spectres from a past so terrible for Cuban culture, but all of us were sure that the unexpected unity among intellectuals caused by these "resurrections" foiled a plan which, although absurd, had a rather sinister smell to it.

Mauricio Vicent, then Cuba correspondent for the Spanish newspaper El País in, in his article "El recuerdo del 'quinquenio gris' moviliza a los intelectuales cubanos" ("Memories of the 'five grey years' mobilises Cuban intellectuals"), on 13 January 2007, summarised it as follows:
"First there were a few friends, who began to phone each other and exchange emails that very night(...) Among the first writers to exchange messages were Jorge Ángel Pérez, Desiderio Navarro, Arturo Arango, Reynaldo González and Antón Arrufat, the latter two "parametrised" and marginalised at that time for their homosexuality, among other "ideological weaknesses". (...) In less than three days, about 40 Cuban intellectuals sent messages of support or testimonies that enlivened and enriched the debate, including writers César López, Sigfredo Ariel, Ena Lucía Portela, Ambrosio Fornet, Waldo Leyva, Jaime Sarusky and Miguel Barnet; playwrights and actors Abelardo Estorino, Pancho García and Carlos Celdrán, filmmakers Enrique Pineda Barnet, Senel Paz and Juan Carlos Tabío, the choreographer Ramiro Guerra, as well as Eliseo Alberto, Amir Valle and Abilio Estévez, and other intellectuals in exile. "

For the first time, we were united in recognising the responsibility we all shared in the national disaster. Desiderio Navarro pointed out that if "politicians' responsibility for limiting intellectuals' critical role" was significant, so was "the intellectuals' responsibility: without the silence and passivity of almost all of them (not to mention the complicity and opportunism of not a few), the "five grey years" or the "Pavonato" as many called it, would not have been possible or, at the very least, it would not have been as destructive". I recall that, as Mauricio Vicent himself mentioned in his article, I asked for a genuine and thorough debate and added that "I hope that the time will come when there are no attempts to free of blame the people guilty of those disasters, and of the many that have been perpetrated since (and are still being perpetrated), and that blame, to be very clear, begins with Fidel and extends to the many Pavóns we know today. That is among the many other points that should be clarified, speaking plainly and without mincing words".

Gerardo Fulleda León, one of the victims of the censorship of El Puente group, recalled that both victims and perpetrators had agreed to keep quiet for three decades, avoiding an issue fundamental to Cuban culture, and he very wisely wrote that this was not the time for "fear, or silence, but for unity to stop any attempt to turn back the clock, so we can prevent history from being repeated".

What was really unprecedented was that, except for a few exceptions when some tried to question the fact that Cuban exiles were adding their messages to the "debate", the whole discussion was focused on the need to prevent the old spectre of cultural repression from ever again haunting the cultural scene. This unity between the two sides (island and exile) on the essence of the problem, together with the unprecedented fact that several generations of Cuban artists had spontaneously formed a common platform for respectful dialogue, laying aside hurts and differences, rang alarm bells with the highest political leaders who, as would later to come to light, ordered the Minister Abel Prieto to put a halt to a snowball that could reach dangerous dimensions.

His Machiavellian strategy was to organise what most of the victims had spent years clamouring for: a forum for the catharsis of their pain.

What happened next is shameful: a commission of the "chosen" visited the Grand Commissar Abel Prieto to call him to account (as one of them would say in another exchange of messages, not even they believed that Abel would answer honestly); a meeting at the Casa de las Américas where none of the "leaders of the protest" complained about the number of colleagues who were refused entry; victims then displayed their wounds in forums with limited space and entry barred to young writers and voices of the opposition; publication of these events, shrouding them in a cloak of deception, presenting them as an act of poetic justice that the Revolution had granted these "revolutionary artists" as proof that these errors would never be repeated; political commissars declaring the case closed in interviews and statements in which, among other ploys, they replaced the stones that had fallen from the wall of division by announcing that Cuban artists and writers, UNEAC and other structures of cultural power had once again won a battle against the "intolerantes" and extremists who, both on the island and in exile, thought they could exploit these developments to mortally wound the Revolution; and finally the publication of the speeches in this "debate" in the book 'La política cultural del periodo revolucionario: Memoria y reflexión' ('The cultural policy of the revolutionary period: Report and reflection'), presented in another "show" at the 2008 International Book Fair, again controlling the audience to avoid potentially dangerous voices.

Although some of participants in this debate were satisfied with licking their wounds public, the debate died, burying mistakes as things of the past, although we all had proof that the same mistakes were still being repeated. The words of Desiderio Navarro in the book are therefore cynical and shameful: "the willingness to remember, clarify, explore, explain, listen, understand and discuss in order to uphold the historical truth and the moral principles that gave rise to and legitimised the Revolution, for which this debate has undoubtedly been a highly anticipated and real triumph of its self-confidence and maturity".

There is more sincerity and common sense in what was said to me, forebodingly, in email exchanges by Ángel Santiesteban, "I have never felt so ashamed to call myself a writer, I never thought that cowardice and writer could sound like the same word and the worst thing is that, from what I can seen, we'll always be dragging around the yoke of domesticated beasts" and novelist Ena Lucía Portela, "Pigs walking happily to slaughter, that's how they've behaved. From now on any repression will be excused and silenced.

They now know that we'll never be able to raise ourselves out of our misery and fear."

EPILOGUE

NEW STRATEGIES FOR THE FUTURE NEO-CASTRO ERA

One of Fidel Castro's best-known "virtues" has been his chameleon-like quality; that intuition which allows him to detect any sign of change in advance and to seamlessly adapt to any circumstances, adverse or favourable. It is to this, which he applied to all areas of his life, including emotional and private, that the Cuban Revolution has owed much of its survival over the past 57 years. Nobody can ever understand what Cuba is today and what the Cuban Revolution has been by ignoring Fidel's complex personality, the transferral of all his vices and idiosyncrasies to the political system that he was moulding and, as a consequence, the forming of a social structure unable to conceive of his infallibility. In simple terms, it is impossible to understand the Cuba of the past five decades without accepting that Castroism is not only a political system but also a philosophy of life. Although it would need another book to explain this issue further, I must add that, without analysing that particular philosophy of life, it will never be possible to understand the real background to the "changes" proposed by Raúl Castro since he took power in 2006; nor to detect the almost invisible thread with which Castroism is guiding the steps of the new leadership – Neo-Castroism – in its succession to the old Castro generation; nor to understand what is different about the Neo-Castroists nor where they have been infected by those autophagous germs that will eventually lead to self-destruction.

The subject of many analyses is something which may seem absurd: like any other element of society that Fidel moulded in his image and likeness, Cuban culture obeys the general objective laws of philosophy, anthropology, politics, etc. only when it is analysed as part of the political ideology of Castroism. As hundreds of studies indicate, culture produced in Cuba in the so-called "revolutionary period", although based on the Stalinist model and repeating some of those mistakes of control, has followed paths, methods and parameters which coincide very little with "Soviet culture". Most of these studies also agree that there is a schism between the culture of Cuba prior to 1959 and the culture of these last 57 years of Castroism. Many supporters of the Revolution, and many naive enemies, believe that Fidel's government before and Raúl's today sincerely aimed to put culture at the service of society and the people. (They support their arguments by referring to the undeniable government support which has helped produce one of the most significant developments in culture in the world, including many First World countries). They usually refer to a word which, in the Cuban context, is an insult to common sense: independence, because in their opinion the Revolution "gave free rein to popular creativity", "culture was made available to the masses as the free expression of any Cuban", "it took culture out of the ivory tower it had inhabited before 1959", "it granted total creative freedom" and other nonsense parroting the dictatorship's propaganda. If everything done to punish me for not becoming a cultural propagandist of "revolutionary" ideology is insufficient proof, I can testify, having been immersed in the world of Cuban culture since the age of 13, that "independence", "creative freedom" and "free expression of creativity" are terms that have applied only in that private and solitary time of artistic creation (in the cases of those who have managed to cure themselves of the virus of self-censorship and fear, undeniably a plague among the island's artists, writers and intellectuals). However, once you decide to share your work in a context where the only master is the government and where "the cultural policy of the Revolution" rules like an inflexible law, these terms: "independence," "creative freedom", "free expression of creativity" are concepts as tangible as EGS-zs8-1, the farthest galaxy, 13 billion light years from earth.

Nobody who wants to understand Cuban culture today can ignore this fact: it is an appendage of the political ideology of Castroism and therefore an instrument of revolutionary propaganda, something that institutions such as UNEAC, the Hermanos Saíz Association, other parts of the Ministry of Culture and the cultural commissars often remind us in their declarations – culture should be "a weapon of the revolution". However, neither is it possible to ignore the role that the "war with the United States" has played, especially in recent times, in shaping that rhetoric of the trenches.

One might think that the President Barack Obama's naivety in breaking with a policy of confrontation for over 50 years between the Cuban and US governments, making unilateral concessions in all areas without demanding anything at all from Raúl Castro, would overturn the rhetoric of a "country besieged by the enemy". However, from Obama's very first conciliatory gestures right up to the present, both the press and the culture propaganda machine have been insisting that there is "a new strategy to put an end to the Revolution". All of the ideologues of the dictatorship are aware of the consequences of what could be the most dangerous of Obama's proposals: that closer contact between the two societies, people to people, would produce many more changes in Cuban society in the short- and long-term than the political confrontation of the past five decades. As some Cuban political commissars have said on television programmes on the subject, the battlefield has become so much more complex that "saving culture from these new methods of interference is to save the Revolution".

While the United States now encourages cultural exchanges (there is a real flow of Cuban and American professionals travelling in both directions to universities and events), and while its university courses are open to young opponents of its administration and dissident members of civil society, it has accepted without protest the Cuban government's unilateral conclusion that this exchange is still marred by ideology and exclusion. Just to mention two examples: the United States does not impose restrictions based on the political affiliations of any of the professionals who travel to their territory under this exchange. However, the government of the island is claiming the right to limit the inclusion of American professionals in programmes and events held in Cuba, accepting only those who openly support the regime, and it also refuses to include in such an exchange a large number of exiled professionals critical of the dictatorship.

In the knowledge that many American intellectuals continue to support the Cuban Revolution out of nostalgia, the cultural commissars (led by Abel Prieto, and at this point it should not be forgotten that he is Raúl Castro's advisor) have stated in many meetings at different levels that the biggest challenge for academics and pro-Party intellectuals is to conquer this sector in the United States which, as we know, has a great impact on American public opinion. It should also be noted that the European Union's clear intention to forge a closer relationship with Cuba, which has already resulted in stronger ties between Europe and Cuba on cultural matters, has meant that this proselytising strategy to attract intellectuals has also spread into European circles.

The political police have joined this effort and know that American intellectuals (even left-wing) usually get frightened when censorship or repression is too obvious. Therefore, to reinforce the image of tolerance towards "enemy" intellectual thinking on the island, they have been camouflaging their methods with a subtlety that manages to confuse even the best-trained intellectuals. To give just one example of these new tactics, I will mention the case of a renowned American anthropologist, an expert in racial issues, who travelled to the island in 2015 to conduct a study on the causes for the decline in the support black people traditionally gave the Revolution in its early years. At his university, he had met "by chance" a young exiled researcher willing to get in contact with another colleague who could get him meetings in Cuba with supposedly "non-Castroist" sources. In the end, these sources provided information that would lead him to conclusions so pro-regime that even he could not believe them, and so he threw away his research.

Within the Castroist cultural bureaucracy, it is well known that any level of management has a free hand to negotiate or make agreements with institutions or figures from other countries which will help promote or reinforce abroad the idea that this is a time of change, openness and tolerance on the island. As it is an established political and propaganda strategy, in many of these cases managers have only to inform their superiors before signing their agreement. However, those same officials are required to meet rigid bureaucratic procedures involving information, analysis and waiting for approval for any event, negotiation or agreement that may constitute an actual change, expression of openness or gesture of tolerance within the country.

In the world of literature there is something strange which, although nobody says that it is part of this strategy, helps its aims. On the island there are two major taboos surrounding how the writer must reflect reality: the first, mostly promoted by the old representatives of the realist school (led by writer Eduardo Heras León, teach of the younger generations of Cuban writers as director of the Onelio Jorge Cardoso National Literary Training Centre) stipulates that before writing, one must always distance oneself from reality or find its "enduring elements", because immediate reality and many specific elements of recent history do not generally result in "great literature". The second taboo is a widespread belief among the old writers who favour the imaginary over reality (a taboo fiercely defended by writers who are members of the Gay Lobby). For them, reality is only a starting point in the search for scenarios where spirituality, polysemy, absurdity and yarn-spinning create a literary world far removed from any trace of a reality which they regard as spiritually empty and vulgar. I have talked in recent years with publishers and literary agents who have gone to Cuba to find novels and they are amazed that most of these works almost entirely avoid traumatic events of everyday life and moments of crisis in social thinking within the country produced by the Castro regime's appalling political and economic governance.

Special mention must be made of the strategy against cultural projects run by Cubans abroad promoting unity between the culture of the island and that of exile. There are the classics ('Diario de Cuba', 'Cubaencuentro') and a group of cultural magazines edited by Cubans which have sporadically received attacks in recent years. 'Linden Lane Magazine', by Belkis Cuza Malé, 'Palabra Abierta' ('Open Word') by Manuel Gayol, and my OtroLunes, a Hispanoamerican culture magazine, could all tell very exciting tales about cyber and other attacks organised from Cuba. Cuban commissars have also made statements at various times against publishers of excellent work such as Fabio Murrieta's Aduana Vieja and Ladislao Aguado's Hypermedia. However, those subject to most attacks are based in Miami. Just to give an example, I think about all that has been done to disrupt Armando Añel and Idabell Rosales' excellent work fronting the NeoClub Press and VISTA Festival, who have had to survive the hacking of their websites. Given the critical seriousness of their proposals, I am convinced that the *Signum Nous* magazine and publishing house, also in Miami, must already be in the sights of the island's cultural commissars.

The Cuban reality is, in short, characterised by a stubborn refusal to accept any idea of change: the publishing houses exert an even greater monopoly over what is published, using the well-worn but effective policy of permitting those works that "play with the chain without yanking the monkey too much"; the "thinkers" propose a review of socialism from within, but based on a "more objective reinterpretation" of Marxism; the official historians have raised the old spectres of annexation and "Yankee" boots grinding in the face of the Cuban people, and try to create a new nationalist discourse to fill the black hole created by the fact that the five decade-old enemy, the United States, now acts as an indulgent friend; the economic crisis affecting the country is the justification for sponsoring only certain (and increasingly few) cultural projects, and those chosen to receive that funding are "by chance" those who best serve the regime's propaganda aims; cultural exchanges with any country must meet the government's political and ideological conditions; the press continues to offer the same trench rhetoric of the worst years of the Cold War, despite attempts by some young journalists who have to settle for a presence in the official blogosphere, permanently controlled by the censors to prevent them going beyond what is officially permitted; in recent times, through the ALBA Cultural project, publication and paid trips off the island for artists, writers, intellectuals and cultural officials showing loyalty to the "revolutionary" ideology are still used as control mechanisms; the political police continues to create an atmosphere of fear among artists in Cuba, especially among those who often travel abroad and have contacts with projects or exiles considered enemies, and it is embarrassing to see the passivity with which most of the island's artists and intellectuals allow their colleagues to be censored and repressed; international fairs have become so politicised that they have been converted into perfect mechanisms for the regime's propaganda; independent projects, whether of the opposition or without links to any political group, are beleaguered, threatened and forced to kowtow or disappear; and there is still a list of thousands of exiled artists banned from visiting the island, although supposedly now all Cubans can enter and leave the country freely.

In reality, nothing has changed: in his speech in 2015 at the end of a session of the Committee on Education, Culture, Science, Technology and Environment of the National Assembly of People's Power (the Cuban parliament), the Cuban Vice-President Miguel Díaz Canel, currently Raúl Castro's most obvious successor in 2018, referred to the new era of relations with the United States. He said, "The opponents of the Cuban process seek to use culture as a platform for restoring capitalism" and that "Cuba must seize the economic opportunities this situation presents, but it must also take up the ideological challenge". On several occasions, like Abel Prieto, Miguel Barnet and other cultural commissars, he stated that "the Revolution has only one cultural policy" – one that began in 1961 when Fidel Castro declared his famous principle "Within the Revolution, everything; against the Revolution, no rights at all".

Berlin, 20 February 2016

ACKNOWLEDGEMENTS

This book would not have been possible without the research, articles and books on the subject and other Cuban cultural issues by, among others (in alpabetical order) Abel Sierra Madero, Alina Brower, Ambrosio Fornet, Ángel Santiesteban Prats, Antonio José Ponte, Armando Añel, Arturo Arias Polo, Beatriz Calvo Peña, Carlos Alberto Montaner, Carlos Espinosa Domínguez, Carlos M. Luis, Daniel Balderston, Desiderio Navarro, Duanel Díaz, Eduardo Heras León, Enrique Colina, Enrique del Risco, Enrique Saínz, Ernesto Hernández Busto, Ernesto Pérez Chang, Gerardo Fernández Fe, Idalia Morejón Arnaiz, Iván de la Nuez, Javier L. Mora, Jesús Díaz, Jesús Hernández Cuéllar, Jesús J. Barquet, Jorge Cabezas Miranda, Jorge Fornet, Jorge Luis Arcos, Jorge Pomar, José Manuel Martín Medem, José Manuel Prieto, Juan Antonio Blanco, Juan Antonio Borrego, Juan Carlos Cremata, Luis de la Paz, Manuel Ballagas, Manuel Díaz Martínez, Manuel Gayol Mecías, Manuel Zayas, María Elena Cruz Varela, Marlies Pahlenberg, Mauricio Vicent, Olga Connor, Orlando Jiménez Leal, Rafael Rojas, Raquel Egea Casas, Reina María Rodríguez, Ricardo Vega, Roberto Zurbano, Seymour Menton, Vicente Botín, Víctor Fowler, Waldo Fernández Cuenca, Wilfredo Cancio Isla and Zoé Valdés.

PREVIOUSLY APPEARED IN THE SERIES
_ Honduras _ Dina Meza, *Kidnapped*
_ Vietnam _ Bui Thanh Hieu, *Speaking in Silence*
_ China _ Sofie Sun, *Drugs for the Mind*
_ Ethiopia _ Bisrat Handiso, *Genocide of Thought*
_ Macedonia _ Tomislav Kezharovski, *Likvidacija/Annihilation*

TO APPEAR THIS SPRING
_ Cuba _ Amir Valle, *Gagged*
_ Cuba _ Amir Valle, *Palabras Amordazadas*
_ Bangladesh _ MD Parvez Alam, *Disappearing Public-Spheres*
_ Turkey _ Fréderike Geerdink, *Bans, Jails and Shameless Lies*
_ Economics _ Peter de Haan, *Censorship Alert*

TO APPEAR IN AUTUMN
_ El Salvador _ Jorge Galán, *The Long Shadow*
_ Surinam _ Sylvana van den Braak, *A Fri Wortu*

The printed titles are available for free via
Janhonout@evatasfoundation.com.
As an ebook via the common outlets.

www.ingramcontent.com/pod-product-compliance
Lightning Source LLC
Chambersburg PA
CBHW060504280326
41933CB00014B/2861